FINANCIAL ASTROLOGY

Almanac 2024

Trading & Investing Using the Planets

M.G. Bucholtz, B.Sc, MBA, M.Sc.

A WOOD DRAGON BOOK

Financial Astrology Almanac 2024
Trading & Investing Using the Planets

Copyright © 2023 by M.G. Bucholtz

Published by:
Wood Dragon Books
Box 429, Mossbank, Saskatchewan, Canada, S0H 3G0
http://www.wooddragonbooks.com

ISBN: 978-1-990863-55-4 (Paperback)
ISBN: 978-1-990863-56-1 (eBook)

Contact the author at: supercyclereport@gmail.com or visit www.investingsuccess.ca

DEDICATION

To the many traders and investors who, at some visceral level, suspect there is more to the financial market system than P/E ratios and analyst recommendations.

You are correct. There is more. Much more. Rooted in astronomical and astrological timing, the markets are a rich tapestry of interwoven cycles. This book will add a whole new dimension to your trading and investing activities.

DISCLAIMER

All material provided herein is based on material gleaned from mathematical and astrological publications researched by the author to supplement his own trading. This publication is written for those who actively trade and invest in the financial markets and who are looking to incorporate astrological phenomena and esoteric math into their market activity. While the material presented herein has proven reliable to the author in his personal trading and investing activity, there is no guarantee this material will continue to be reliable into the future.

The author and publisher assume no liability whatsoever for any investment or trading decisions made by readers of this book. The reader alone is responsible for all trading and investment outcomes and is further advised not to exceed his or her risk tolerances when trading or investing in the financial markets.

TABLE OF CONTENTS

INTRODUCTION

Many traders and investors think company media releases, media news opinions, quarterly earnings reports, and analyst targets drive stock prices and major index movements. I disagree.

I believe price action is driven by human emotion. Psychologists describe six emotions: happy, sad, fear, disgust, anger, and surprise. I have a shorter list. I believe fear and greed are the two broad classes of emotion that influence the financial markets. When we are greedy, we run towards the market. We buy, buy, buy. When we are fearful, we run away from the market. We sell, sell, sell.

I believe the emotions of fear and greed are particularly influenced by events in our cosmos such as changes in planetary declination of Venus and Mars, angular aspects between orbiting planets, perihelion and aphelion occurrences of Mercury and Venus, and heliocentric intervals of planetary movement.

I further believe that of all the celestial bodies, the Moon is the most influential. In 1937, New York-based astrologer Louise McWhirter penned a book entitled *The McWhirter Theory of Stock Market Forecasting.* In her book she made clear that the Moon orbiting past certain degree points of the zodiac wheel could trigger price responses on the Dow Jones Average and on individual stocks as well.

Overlap and weave together these celestial phenomena and the result will be the ups and downs of price that characterize a stock chart, a commodity price chart, or the chart of a major index. The average trader or investor who remains fixated on media releases and analyst opinions ignores this rich tapestry of planetary influence.

Distances of planets from the Sun, changes in planetary declination, and movement of the Moon are all astronomy type events. The question that must be dispensed with is–why is the term *astrology* used in the title of this publication? Why is this book not entitled the Financial Astronomy Almanac?

Webster's dictionary states that: *astronomy is concerned with the study of objects outside the earth's atmosphere.* Webster's further says that: *astrology is the divination of how planets influence our lives.*

Years ago, when I first began writing these annual almanacs, I thought about using the word *astronomy*. However, the community of people who apply the study of cosmic events to the financial markets call themselves financial astrologers. So, in keeping with that usage, I have maintained the use of the term *astrology* in the title of my annual publications.

When I began to embrace financial astrology in 2012, it was a monumental shift for me. My educational background includes an Engineering degree, an MBA degree, and a M.Sc. degree. My approach to financial astrology and to the markets in general is thus heavily slanted towards Fibonacci mathematics, quantum science, Kabbalah ratios rooted in the Hebrew Alef-Bet, and cyclical planetary events.

My approach also entails the use of technical chart indicators to help identify changes in price trend. Trend changes that occur at the same time as a cyclical planetary event get my attention quickly. For example, trend changes that occur at Fibonacci price retracements of 48.6%, 68.2%, or 78.6% tend to be significant. Trend changes that occur at quantum price lines are always powerful events. Trend changes that occur at heliocentric degree advances (137.5, 150.5, 209.5, or 222.5 degrees as calculated using Kabbalah math) of Mars or Venus from a significant price high or low also tend to be significant.

I cannot emphasize enough the importance of following the price trend when trading and investing. So strong is my conviction towards the trend, in 2023 I released a book entitled *Follow the Trend—When to Buy and When to Sell*. Of all the trend indicators discussed in the book, the *Ergodic Oscillator* and the *True Strength Index* are particularly powerful. Both were developed by trader and mathematician William Blau in the 1980s. In addition, the stochastic chart indicators created by Martin Pring and George Lane are also potent. In this edition of the Almanac, I have added a chapter to further explain how to use these various chart indicators.

The *Financial Astrology Almanac 2024* is structured around long cycles, medium cycles, and shorter cycles. A long cycle of planetary activity that overlaps and interweaves with time is the Jupiter/Saturn Gann Master Cycle which unfolds over two decades of heliocentric planetary movement. Threaded through the fabric of this Master Cycle is another long cycle, the McWhirter 18.6-year cycle which aligns to the movement of the North Node through the signs of the zodiac. This nodal cycle broadly defines overall economic activity. As the Node progresses through the zodiac, aspects to major outer planets can exacerbate (or mitigate) the tenor of economic activity.

On a more moderate timeframe, the repeated cyclical movement of Venus and Mars above and below the ecliptic plane aligns to swing highs and swing lows on commodity futures and equity indices. Events of Mercury or Venus being retrograde often align to trend reversals on stocks and equity indices. A similar observation holds for both Mercury and Venus being at easterly and westerly elongation extremes, superior conjunctions, inferior conjunctions, perihelion, and aphelion. Medium-term cycles also arise from key annual celebratory events delineated in the Hebrew lunar-based calendar, including the seven-year Shemitah cycles.

On a shorter timeframe, the movement of the Moon through the signs of the zodiac is a powerful phenomenon. Times when the Moon is *Void of Course* align to expressions of notable volatility on equity indices. The cycle from one New Moon to the next can also be seen to have a bearing on the New York Stock Exchange (NYSE), especially when the Moon transits past 14 degrees of Cancer and 24 degrees of Pisces. These degree positions mark the location of the Ascendant and Mid-Heaven respectively on May 17, 1792 when the NYSE was founded. These degree positions also mark the location of the Ascendant and Mid-Heaven on the morning of April 30, 1789–the day George Washington was sworn in as America's first President.

Even though the North American mainstream media refuses to embrace cosmic events as valid tools for timing the markets, it is my opinion that there are powerful players in the major financial centres of the globe who *do* embrace planetary cycles. Knowing that planetary aspects and cycles influence human emotion, these power players use these occurrences to their advantage to make money in up-trending markets. They also use their short-selling prowess at these cyclic events to induce trend reversals on markets. As the price trend turns and markets start to fall, these players profit from their short positions while the average investor on the street experiences emotional angst and sleepless nights knowing the markets are trending down and working against them. "Who are the powerful players that use astrology to move markets?" is a question that burns in my mind. Is it a select group at J.P. Morgan? Is it a group in a dark-panelled office in London? I will likely never know.

How and why these various cosmic events influence human emotion are two other burning questions that remain unanswered. As I have studied these cosmic events over the past dozen years and applied them to the financial markets, I have developed a new sense of awe for what I deem to be a higher power that guides the Universe.

Consider the beliefs of the Cree First Nations people in Alberta, Canada. They pass down through the generations the story of the Pleiades star cluster, visible in the constellation Taurus. One day, Sky Woman spotted a far-away planet and expressed a desire to visit it. Spider Woman, who lived amongst the stars of the Pleiades, spun a web so that Sky Woman could reach the far-off planet. The far-off planet was Earth. Mankind originates with Sky Woman and her visit to Earth. I am often humbled when I look at stock market reactions as Sun, Venus, and Mars transit conjunct to the Pleiades star cluster in Taurus.

Consider the beliefs of the ancient Egyptians with respect to the star Sirius. I am humbled when I look at stock market reactions during periods when Sirius is rising in the early morning sky or setting in the evening sky. After reading this Almanac, you too may have reason to pause and ponder the power of the cosmos. You may well find yourself thinking that a higher power guides the Universe.

Ancient civilizations as far back as the Babylonians recognized planetary cyclical activity, but in a more rudimentary form. Their high priests tracked and recorded changes in the emotions of the people. These diviners and seers also tracked events, both fortuitous and disastrous. Although they lacked the ability to fully comprehend the celestial mechanics of the planetary system, they were able to visually spot the planets Mercury, Venus, Mars, Jupiter, and Saturn in the heavens. They correlated changes in human emotion and societal events to these planets. They assigned to these planets the names of the various deities revered by the people. They identified and named various star constellations in the heavens and divided the heavens into twelve signs. This was the birth of *astrology* as we know it today.

Stories of traders benefiting from planetary activity are also not new. In the early 1900s, esoteric thinkers such as the famous Wall Street trader W.D. Gann reportedly made massive gains when he realized that cycles of astrology bore a striking correlation to financial market price action. Gann is most famous for identifying the Saturn/Jupiter cycle which he labelled the Gann Master Cycle. He followed the cyclical activity of Jupiter and Neptune when he traded Wheat and Corn futures. He also delved deep into esoteric math, notably square root math which led him to develop his Square of Nine approach to trading. The concept of price squaring with time is also a Gann construct. Today many traders and investors attempt to emulate Gann but they do so in a linear fashion, looking for repetitive cycles on the calendar. What they are missing is the astrology component, which is anything but linear.

In the 1930s, Louise McWhirter greatly illuminated the connection between the stock market and planetary cycles. She identified an 18.6-year cyclical correlation between the general state of the American economy and the position of the North Node of the Moon in the zodiac. Her methodology extended to include the transiting Moon passing by key points of the 1792 natal birth horoscope of the New York Stock Exchange. She also identified a correlation between price movement of a stock and those times when transiting Sun, Mars, Jupiter and Saturn made hard aspects to the natal Sun position in the stock's natal birth (first trade) horoscope. [1]

The late 1940s saw planetary mathematical modelling applied to the stock market when astrologer Garth Allen (a.k.a. Donald Bradley) created his *Siderograph Model* based on aspects between the various transiting planets. Each aspect as it occurs is given a sinusoidal weighting as the orb (separation) between the planets varies. Bradley's model was obscured in the aftermath of the 2008 financial crisis when the Federal Reserve started injecting massive amounts of liquidity into the financial system. Now that excess liquidity has stopped flooding the system and the Federal Reserve has embarked on balance sheet reduction, Bradley's model is again proving itself a powerful indicator of trend changes on the S&P 500. [2]

As the 1950s dawned, academics at institutions like Yale and Harvard came to dominate discussions of the financial markets. Talk of planetary cycles influencing financial markets was soon replaced by academic constructs like *Modern Portfolio Theory* and the *Efficient Market Hypothesis*. These models promoted the idea that investing was for the long term and that investors should buy, hold, and forget about the ups and downs of the market. These models persisted for several decades until coming under severe scrutiny first with the 2000 tech bubble meltdown and again with the 2008 sub-prime mortgage collapse that nearly derailed the global economy.

In the past decade, the application of planetary science to the stock market has been elevated and made more user friendly. The software designers at Australian company *Optuma* now have an impressive financial astrology platform built into their charting program. This is the software I have used to generate the charts in this Almanac.

You have probably experienced the effects of the planets on the financial market without even realizing it. Think back to the dark days of late 2008 when there was genuine concern over the very survival of the financial market system. This timeframe was the end of an 18.6-year cycle of the

North Node traveling around the zodiac. To high-level, power-players in the financial system who understood astrology, this period was a prime opportunity to feast off the fear of the investing public and the anxiety of government officials who were standing at the ready with lucrative bailout packages. The market low in March 2009 came at a confluence of a Mars and a Neptune quantum point. (Curiously enough, Mars and Neptune are deemed to be the planetary rulers of the New York Stock Exchange.) The March 2009 low also aligned perfectly to the start of Venus being retrograde.

Think back to August 2015 and the market selloff that the financial media did not see coming. This selloff started at a confluence of three events: Venus being retrograde, the appearance of Venus as a Morning Star after having been only visible as an Evening Star for the previous 263 days, and the close conjunction of Venus and Jupiter (a once in 26-month cyclical event).

Remember the early days of 2016 when Mercury was retrograde and the markets hit a rough patch? Remember the weakness of June 2016 when Venus emerged from conjunction to become visible as an Evening Star?

Do you recall the dire predictions for financial market calamity following the 2016 election of Donald Trump to the White House? When the markets instead powered higher, analysts were flummoxed. Venus was making its declination minima right at the time of the American election. Venus declination minima events bear a striking correlation to changes of trend on US equity markets.

What about the early days of 2018 when fear once again gripped the system? Venus was at its declination minimum. Markets reached another turning point in the first week of October 2018 when Venus was again at a declination low. Add the fact that Venus turned retrograde at the same time and the fear starts to make sense. Markets sold off sharply into mid-December before starting to recover. Sun was conjunct Saturn at this time which correlates strongly to trend changes on equity markets. The North Node had also just changed zodiac signs, an event which also aligns with trend changes.

Markets hit a sudden rough patch in early August 2019 when the Federal Reserve cut interest rates due to overnight repurchase agreement (repo) market liquidity concerns. At the time, Mercury had just finished retrograde and Moon had just transited a key point on the NYSE 1792 natal horoscope.

US equity markets peaked in late February 2020 and went into total spasm in March 2020 when fears of the potential for a viral pandemic were stirred up. At the time, Mercury was retrograde and Mars had just made its declination minimum. Venus was at the same degree of declination it had been in 1792 when the NYSE was founded.

Do you recall the confusion surrounding the November 2020 election of Joe Biden to the White House? The day of the election, Mercury finished retrograde and heliocentric Jupiter and Saturn were exactly at 0-degrees of separation. To have these two specific events occur on the day of the election is a rarity. The events concerning the validity of this election will be hotly debated for years to come.

The events of late 2021 reminded us all again of the power of planetary events. As 2021 was ending, the equity markets were peaking. Mercury was approaching its greatest easterly elongation. Venus was retrograde and also was approaching its inferior conjunction. Mercury would soon turn retrograde. Mars was approaching its declination minimum. This was a concentration of cosmic energy at work. The powerful players (whoever they were) took full advantage, pushing the markets into a downtrend through aggressive selling. Individual investors (whose emotions were rattled by the cosmic events) panicked and started to feed into the downtrend. By June 2022, the selling had caused a full 20% decline across equity markets.

The period September 2021 to September 2022 was a Shemitah Year in the Hebrew faith (a one-in-seven-year occurrence). I predicted at the outset that this Shemitah Year would deliver some headline events. And sure enough, Russia invaded Ukraine, inflation surged, gasoline prices at the pump jumped, and Europe stumbled into an energy crisis. True to form for a Shemitah year, North American markets recorded a significant bottom in October 2022 just after the Shemitah year ended.

Cosmic events continue to unfold as time marches on. People who view the markets through the lens of analyst opinions and media blather will be unable to appreciate this activity hidden in plain view. They will ride an emotional roller coaster as their financial planners tell them that investing is for the long-term and not to worry. On the other hand, investors who are able to identify and appreciate cosmic activity will be able to take steps to protect themselves and profit accordingly.

This Almanac, which is my eleventh such annual publication, is designed to provide a new perspective on the financial markets. I sincerely hope that the material presented herein will help you take your trading and investing activity to a new level. I further hope this Almanac will help you better navigate all the market events that 2024 has in store.

Note from the Author: I am also the author of several other astrology books and publish two bi-weekly subscription-based newsletters called *The Astrology Letter* and *The Cycle Report*. Through all of my written efforts, I hope to encourage people to embrace the events in our cosmos as valuable tools to aid in trading and investing decision making.

CHAPTER ONE

Fundamentals

The Sun is at the center of our solar system, with the Earth, Moon, planets and other asteroid bodies completing the planetary system. In addition to the Sun and Moon, there are eight celestial bodies important to the application of cosmic events to the financial markets. These planets are: Mercury, Venus, Mars, Jupiter, Saturn, Uranus, Neptune, and Pluto.

Figure 1-1 illustrates these various bodies and their spatial relation to the Sun. Mercury is the closest to the Sun while Pluto is the farthest away.

Their distances from the Sun (in astronomical units (au), where 1 au is approximately 150 million km) are: Mercury (0.39 au), Venus (0.79 au), Mars (1.52 au), Jupiter (5.2 au), Saturn (9.54 au), Uranus (19.2 au), Neptune (30.06 au), and Pluto (39 au). Close examination of ratios of these distances to one another shows a close alignment to the Fibonacci sequence. Price retracements that align to Fibonacci ratios, and spatial relations between planets that align to the Fibonacci sequence are both humbling phenomena that lead to the observation – as above, so below.

The Ecliptic and the Zodiac

The various planets and other asteroid bodies rotate 360-degrees around the Sun following a path called the *ecliptic plane*. As shown in Figure 1-2, Earth and its Equator are slightly tilted (approximately 23.45-degrees) relative to the ecliptic plane.

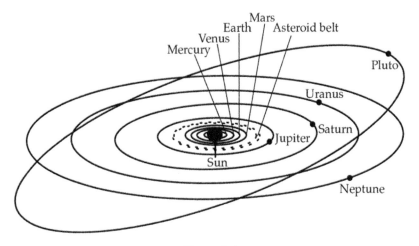

Figure 1-1
The Planets

Projecting the Earth's equator into space produces the *celestial equator plane*. There are two points of intersection between the ecliptic plane and celestial equator plane. Mathematically, this makes sense as two non-parallel planes must intersect at two points. These points are commonly called the *vernal equinox* (occurring at March 20th) and the *autumnal equinox* (occurring at September 20th).

The starting point (or zero-degree point) of the zodiac wheel occurs in the sign Aries at the vernal equinox. The vernal equinox is when, from our vantage point on Earth, the Sun appears at 0-degrees Aries. The Sun at this location is more commonly referred to as the *first day of spring*. The autumnal equinox is when, from our vantage point on Earth, the Sun appears at 180-degrees from the vernal equinox (0-degrees of Libra). Sun at 0-degrees of Libra is more commonly referred to as the *first day of autumn*.

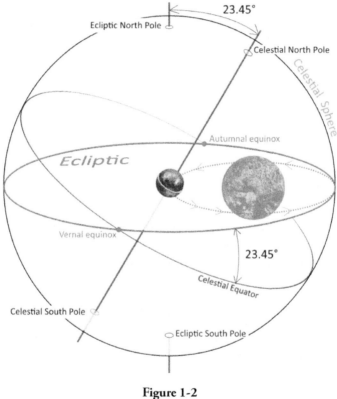

Figure 1-2
The Ecliptic

The Glyphs

Dividing the ecliptic plane into twelve equal sections of 30-degrees results in what astrologers call the *zodiac* or the *zodiac wheel*. Ancient civilizations looking skyward identified patterns of stars called constellations that aligned to these twelve zodiac divisions. The twelve portions of the zodiac have names such as Aries, Cancer, and Leo. (If these names sound familiar, they should. You routinely see all twelve names in the daily horoscope section of your morning newspaper.)

Figure 1-3 illustrates the symbols that appear in the twelve segments of a zodiac wheel. The twelve segments are more properly called *signs*; the symbols are called *glyphs*. The various planets are also denoted by glyphs, as shown in Figure 1-4.

Geocentric and Heliocentric Astrology

The terms *synodic* and *sidereal* help define the two distinct varieties of astrology – geocentric and heliocentric.

In *geocentric* astrology (synodic), the Earth is the vantage point for observing the planets as they pass through the signs of the zodiac.

In *heliocentric* astrology (sidereal), the Sun is the vantage point for observing the planets as they pass through the signs of the zodiac. An observer positioned on the Sun would also see the orbiting planets making aspects with one another.

To identify these aspects, astrologers use Ephemeris tables. For geocentric astrology, the *New American Ephemeris for the 21st Century* is commonly used. For heliocentric astrology, the *American Heliocentric Ephemeris* is a good resource.

Figure 1-3
The Zodiac Wheel

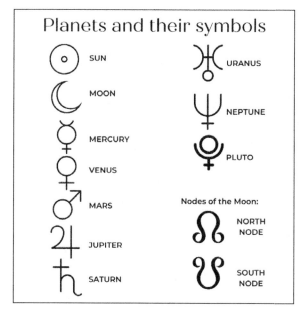

Figure 1-4
The Glyphs

Declination

As the various celestial bodies make their respective journeys around the Sun, they can be seen to move above and below the ecliptic plane. This movement is termed *declination*. Celestial bodies experience declinations of up to about 25-degrees above and below the ecliptic plane. Declination occurs as a result of the Sun's force of gravitational pull on a planet. The larger outer planets (Jupiter, Saturn, Neptune, Uranus and Pluto), owing to their size and distance from the Sun, experience declination changes that are slower to evolve. The smaller inner planets (Mercury, Venus, Mars) exhibit more amplitude in their declination patterns.

Declination is often incorrectly described by financial astrology writers and bloggers. The **correct** way of describing declination is using heliocentric data. An observer situated on a fixed reference point of the Sun will be able to see the various planets moving above or below the ecliptic plane. Attempting to describe declination using geocentric data is misleading because an Earth-bound observer is trying to observe the other planets moving relative to the ecliptic plane is himself moving because the planet Earth is moving above or below the ecliptic.

As this almanac will illustrate, changes in the declination of a celestial body (most notably Mars and Venus) can affect the financial markets. W.D. Gann believed that the dates Venus and Mars return to the same declination level they were at when a stock or a commodity future first started trading (first trade date/natal declination level) can align to price trend changes.

Latitude

As the various celestial bodies make their respective journeys around the Sun, they will sometimes move above or below the celestial equator line (the Earth's equator extended into space). As viewed from Earth, the distance above or below this celestial equator line is a planet's *latitude*.

Planetary Location

We are accustomed to expressing the location of something in terms of latitude and longitude coordinates. For example, the city of New York is located 40.7 degrees north of the equator and 74 degrees west of Greenwich, England (the Prime Meridian). Planets can also be described using a coordinate system.

An observer situated on the Sun wishing to describe the coordinates of a particular planet would express the coordinates in terms of declination and longitude. That is, where in the 360-degree circle (longitude) is the planet and how much is it above or below the ecliptic plane (declination).

An observer situated on Earth wishing to describe the coordinates of a particular planet would express the coordinates in terms of latitude and *right ascension* (RA). The units of measure for RA are hours and minutes where one hour is equivalent to a 15-minute segment of our 360-degree cosmos. (15-minute segments x 24 segments = 360 degrees.)

Aspects

Owing to the different times for the planets to each orbit the Sun, an observer situated on Earth will see the planets making distinct angles (called *aspects*) with one another and also with the Sun. An observer situated on the Sun, will see the planets making distinct angles (called *aspects*) with one another and also with the Earth. The aspects that are commonly used in mundane astrology are 0, 30, 45, 60, 90, 120, 150 and 180-degrees. In financial astrology, it is common to refer to only the 0, 90, 120 and 180-degree aspects.

Data

Instead of using an Ephemeris book of tabular data, quicker aspect determination can be made using software. An excellent software program is *Solar Fire Gold* produced by software company Astrolabe. I also use a market platform called *Optuma/Market Analyst*. This brilliant piece of software, developed in Australia, allows the user to generate end-of-day price charts for equities and commodities from a multitude of exchanges and then overlay various planetary aspects and cyclical planetary occurrences onto the chart. As your journey into trading and investing using the planets deepens, you might be tempted to spend the money to acquire a software program.

The Moon

Just as the planets orbit 360-degrees around the Sun, the Moon orbits 360-degrees around the Earth. The Moon orbits the Earth in a plane of motion called the *lunar ecliptic plane*. This plane is inclined at about 5-degrees to the ecliptic plane as Figure 1-5 shows. The Moon orbits Earth with a slight elliptical pattern in approximately 27.3 days, relative to an observer located on a fixed frame of reference such as the Sun. This time period is known as a *sidereal month*. However, during one sidereal month, an observer located on Earth (a moving frame of reference) will revolve part way around the Sun. Because of this added movement, the Earth-bound observer will see a complete orbit of the Moon around the Earth in approximately 29.5 days. This 29.5-day period of time is known as a *synodic month* or more commonly a *lunar* month. The lunar month plays a key role in discerning the volatility of the financial markets.

The Nodes

A mathematical construct related to the Moon, and central to financial markets, is the *Nodes*. The Nodes are the points of intersection between the Earth's ecliptic plane and the Moon's ecliptic plane. In astrology, typically only the North Node is referred to. The North Node forms the basis for the McWhirter Method which will be discussed in Chapter 3.

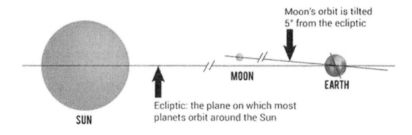

Figure 1-5
Lunar Orbit

Synodic and Sidereal Cycles

The concepts of synodic and sidereal also extend beyond the Moon to include all the planets. To an earth-bound observer, a synodic time period is the time between two successive planetary occurrences. That is, how many days does it take for Sun passing Pluto on the zodiac wheel to Sun again passing Pluto? To a Sun-bound observer (a fixed frame of reference), a sidereal time period is the number of days (or years) it takes for a planet to orbit the Sun. The table in Figure 1-6 presents synodic and sidereal data.

PLANET	SYNODIC PERIOD	SIDEREAL PERIOD
Mercury	116 days	88 days
Venus	584 days	225 days
Mars	780 days	1.9 years
Jupiter	399 days	11.9 years
Saturn	378 days	29.5 years
Uranus	370 days	84 years
Neptune	368 days	164.8 years
Pluto	367 days	248.5 years

Figure 1-6
Synodic and Sidereal Data

Ascendant, Descendant, Medium Coeli, and Imum Coeli

As the Earth rotates on its axis once in every 24 hours, an observer situated on Earth will detect an apparent motion of the constellation stars that define the zodiac. To better define this motion, astrologers apply four cardinal points to the zodiac, almost like the north, south, east and west points on a compass. These cardinal points divide the zodiac into four quadrants. The east point is termed the *Ascendant* and is often abbreviated *Asc*. The west point is termed the *Descendant* and is often abbreviated Dsc. The south point is termed the Medium Coeli (Latin for *Mid Heaven*) and is often abbreviated *MC* or *MH*. The north point is termed the *Imum Coeli* (Latin for *bottom of the sky*) and is abbreviated *IC*. The two cardinal points most often used in this Almanac are the Ascendant and the Mid-Heaven.

Figure 1-7 illustrates the placement of these cardinal points on a typical zodiac wheel. In Figure 1-7, Ascendant and Imum Coeli are both situated 90-degrees from the Ascendant. There are several ways of dividing the zodiac wheel into its divisions. The ecliptic plane itself can be divided into segments. Or, the celestial equator plane can be divided into segments which are then projected onto the ecliptic plane. (*The*

Placidus system of divisions will be used when the importance of the Ascendant and Mid-Heaven in the context of the McWhirter Method is discussed in Chapter 3.)

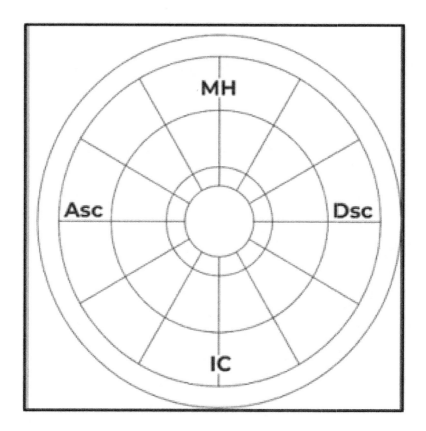

Figure 1-7
Cardinal Points

Retrograde

The term retrograde is taken from the Latin expression retrogradus which means "backward step."

From our vantage point on Earth, we describe the position of the planets relative to one of the twelve constellations in the sky. There will be three (occasionally four) times during a year when Earth and Mercury pass by each other (Mercury retrograde). There will be one time (occasionally two times) per year when Earth and Venus pass each other (Venus retrograde). There will be one time every two years when Earth and Mars pass each other (Mars retrograde). In the case of a faster-moving planet starting to lap past slower-moving Earth, we can observe the faster-planet's position relative to one of the star constellations in the sky. Owing to the different orbital speeds of Earth and the faster planet, there will be a period of time when we see the faster planet in what appears to be the previous constellation. For example, we might start off seeing Mercury against the star constellation of Gemini. As Mercury begins to lap past Earth, we will see Mercury against the star constellation of Taurus. As Mercury passes by Earth, we will see Mercury again in Taurus. Of course, Mercury has not physically reversed course and moved backwards. This is an optical illusion created by the different orbital speeds of Mercury and Earth.

These brief illusory periods are what astrologers call retrograde events. To ancient societies, retrograde events were of great significance as human emotion was often seen to be changeable at these events.

Retrograde events involving Mercury, Venus, and Mars very often lead to short term price trend changes developing. Is it possible that our DNA is hard-wired such that we feel uncomfortable at retrograde events? Does this emotional discomfort compel us to buy or sell on the financial markets?

Elongation and Conjunction

From an observer's vantage point on Earth, there will also be times when planets are at maximum angles of separation from the Sun. These events are what astronomers refer to as maximum easterly and maximum westerly elongations. These events definitely have a correlation to trend changes on the markets.

Mercury and Venus are closer to the Sun than is the Earth. From our vantage point on Earth, there will be times when Mercury and Venus are situated between the Earth and the Sun. There will also be times when the Sun is between the Earth and Mercury or Venus. On the zodiac wheel, the times when Mercury or Venus are in the same zodiac sign and degree as the Earth are what astronomers call conjunctions.

An inferior conjunction occurs when Mercury or Venus is between Earth and the Sun.

A superior conjunction occurs when the Sun is between Earth and Mercury or Venus. Figure 1-8 illustrates the concept of elongation and conjunction.

Inferior conjunction events occur on either side of retrograde events. For example, Venus was retrograde from December 19, 2021 through January 28, 2022. Its exact Inferior Conjunction was recorded on January 8, 2022. The peak on the S&P 500 in early January 2022 was directly connected to these Venus phenomena which disturbed human emotion. As unsettled investors began selling, the trend on the S&P 500 changed to negative. The negative sentiment remained intact until mid-June 2022 when the Sun recorded its declination maximum. Following this brief reprieve, the trend soon shifted back to negative. Such are the intricacies of the cosmos and their effects on human emotion and the markets.

After Venus has been at inferior conjunction, it will be visible in the early morning hours as the *Morning Star.*

After it has been at superior conjunction, it will be visible just before sunset as the *Evening Star.*

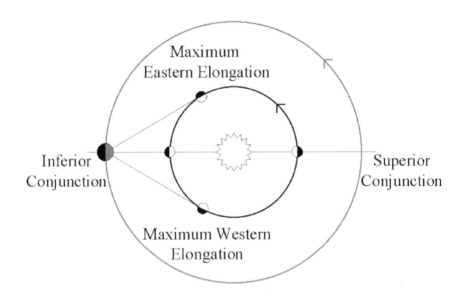

Figure 1-8
Superior and Inferior Conjunction

Venus was at Superior Conjunction on March 28, 2013 (8 Aries), October 25, 2014 (1 Scorpio), June 6, 2016 (16 Gemini), January 8, 2018 (18 Capricorn), August 14, 2019 (20 Leo), March 26, 2021 (6 Aries), and October 22, 2022 (28 Libra).

Venus was at inferior conjunction on June 6, 2012 (15 Gemini), January 11, 2014 (21 Capricorn), August 15, 2015 (22 Leo), March 25, 2017 (4 Aries), October 26, 2018 (3 Scorpio), June 3, 2020 (14 Gemini), and January 8, 2022 (19 Capricorn).

If one plots consecutive superior conjunction events (or consecutive inferior conjunction events) on a zodiac wheel, the plot points can be joined to form a 5-pointed star called a pentagram. Such is the elegance and mystique of the cosmos.

Moon Void of Course (VOC)

The Moon moves through a sign of the zodiac every 2.5 days. Often, there will be a short period of time just before the Moon enters a new sign where it makes no aspects to any of the planets in the zodiac. This brief timeframe is referred to as Moon Void of Course (VOC). It is not uncommon to see emotions temporarily become heightened and markets become jittery at these void of course events. In a given month, the Moon will be VOC approximately 12 times. In order for VOC to affect equity markets, the VOC event must occur between Monday and Friday, must be more than four hours in duration, and must occur during NYSE trading hours. I disregard any VOC events outside these parameters. The net result is that in a typical month there might be up to four VOC events that affect the markets.

Having looked at these basics, let's next engage in a deeper exploration of events of the cosmos and how these events can impact financial markets.

CHAPTER TWO

Trend Changes

In previous editions of this Almanac, I have included a paragraph advising readers that planetary cyclical events should be acted on if a price trend change is also visible on the stock, commodity future, or index being studied. Discussions with people who have purchased previous Almanacs, or who subscribe to my newsletters, have revealed that the subject of trend change needs more focus in my written offerings. This chapter focuses on price trend and illustrates how technical chart indicators can be used to help determine when the price trend changes.

Financial market data platforms come programmed with a variety of *moving averages* ranging from *simple* to *exponential* to *smoothed*.

On a given trading day, the *simple moving average* is the mathematical average of the past *'n'* price bars on a price chart of a stock, commodity, or futures contract. The next day, the calculations discard the first value in the data series and add the most recent data point. There is considerable flexibility in determining how many data points to use in the average calculation. I regard the 200-day moving average to be indicative of the broader trend. I regard the 50-day moving average to be indicative of the shorter-term trend. The trend can be deemed to be changing from bearish to bullish when price moves up and through a moving average. Similarly, the trend is turning bearish when price moves below a moving average.

An *exponential* moving average is similar to a simple moving average, except the mathematical calculation underlying the exponential average places greater weight (emphasis) on the more recent of the *'n'* data points.

A *smoothed* moving average is an average of an average. Suppose an 18-day moving average has been calculated using n=18 price bars. After a longer period of time has elapsed, suppose an 18-day moving average of a series of 18-day moving average data points is calculated. This smoothed moving average reduces the variability of the data points and helps traders better identify trend directions.

Market data platforms also come programmed with a variety of *stochastic* and *oscillator* functions. Stochastic and oscillator functions compute the price range of data over a specified period of time. The price at a given day is then expressed as a percentage of this data range. I have a preference for the Ergodic Oscillator and the True Strength Index, both developed in the 1990s by trader and mathematician William Blau. Not every data platform will provide the *Ergodic Oscillator,* but certainly the *True Strength Index* will be a standard offering.

Consider the example of energy producer Devon Energy (NYSE: DVN) in Figure 2-1. As of late September 2023, the prevailing trend was bearish with price beneath the 200-day average and also beneath the 50-day average. Notice how the price periodically rallied towards the 50-day average and in some cases surpassed the average. A trader seeking to take advantage of these counter-trend moves in price could have used crossovers of the True Strength Index to identify buying opportunities.

Figure 2-1
Devon Energy (NYSE:DVN)

Figure 2-2 illustrates price action on chipmaker Micron Technology (NYSE:MU). As of late September 2023, the prevailing trend was bullish with price having crossed above the 200-day average in March. Although the broader trend had been bullish, notice how the price periodically fell beneath the 50-day average only to recover and move above the average. A trader seeking to take advantage of these counter-trend moves in price could have used the True Strength Index to identify buying opportunities.

I also use the *Slow Stochastic Oscillator*. This oscillator function was developed by famed market trader George Lane in the early 1960s. The oscillator function comprises an indicator line and a signal line. The indicator line crossing over the signal line generates a buy signal. I pay particular attention to these crossovers when they occur at an oscillator value less than 20. When the oscillator surpasses its upper boundary value of 80 and then crosses beneath this level, a sell signal is triggered.

Figure 2-2
Micron Technology (NYSE:MU)

Figure 2-3 illustrates price action on artificial intelligence company C3ai (NYSE:AI). The price chart has been fitted with the Slow Stochastic indicator. In late April 2023, price found support at the 200-day average. The stochastic was beneath the lower boundary value of 20. A trader buying the stock at this point would have realized slight gains initially. However, once price surpassed the 50-day average, bullish momentum accelerated. A trader would have been wise to heed the oversold stochastic level but then wait for price to surpass the 50-day average before buying the stock. Compare this behavior to what happened in August 2023. The stochastic was beneath the lower boundary of 20. When the indicator line crossed the signal line, price began to move higher. However, the price never did get above the 50-day average. A trader would have been wise to steer clear of buying the stock. Note that as of late September, price breached the 200-day average to signal a bearish trend.

Figure 2-3
C3ai (NYSE:AI)

To delve deeper into the mathematics of the trend, I encourage you to get a copy of my 2023 publication *Follow the Trend*. I explore a wide variety of trend indicators as well as Fibonacci mathematics to help the reader more thoroughly grasp the concept of price trend.

CHAPTER THREE

Long Cycles

The Gann Master Cycle

W.D. Gann closely followed the cycles of Jupiter and Saturn. To an observer situated on the fixed (heliocentric) vantage point of the Sun, Jupiter can be seen orbiting the Sun in about 12 years and Saturn in just over 29 years. Gann interpreted these orbital cycles one step further and noted that every 19.86 years, heliocentric Jupiter and Saturn were at conjunction (separated by 0-degrees) in a particular sign of the zodiac. This 19.86-year time span is what he called the *Master Cycle*.

The curious feature of the Master Cycle is that the occurrence of the Jupiter/Saturn conjunction does not always align precisely with a change of trend. Following a conjunction event, market price action can sometimes re-test the price lows made at the conjunction event. Consider the following examples:

✪ The market weakness in late 1901 aligned to a conjunction of these two outer planets. But following this conjunction event, the Dow Jones did not reach a definitive turning point low until late 1903 when the two planets were 45-degrees apart.

✪ In 1920, the U.S. economy encountered a recession. In August 1921, Jupiter and Saturn reached conjunction. After conjunction, the Dow Jones started to rally higher almost as if on queue. The Dow Jones severely re-tested the 1921 lows in 1932 when the two planets were exactly 150-degrees apart.

✪ In late 1940, Jupiter and Saturn again were at conjunction. The Dow Jones did not record a definitive low until early 1942 when the two planets were 30-degrees apart.

✪ In April 1961, Jupiter and Saturn again were at conjunction. The Dow Jones eventually reached a turning point low in mid-1962 when the two planets were 22.5-degrees apart.

✪ In the Spring of 1981, Jupiter and Saturn recorded a conjunction event. The actual market peak came a few months ahead of the exact conjunction when the two planets were 1-degree apart. It would not be until August 1982 that the Dow Jones recorded a turning point low that evolved into a massive bull market run that endured until the next conjunction event in June 2000.

✪ In June of 2000, Jupiter and Saturn recorded a conjunction event. The market peak had already been recorded in January when the two planets were 8-degrees apart. Following this June 2000 conjunction and the start of a new Master Cycle, it would not be until October 2002 that the Dow Jones reached a turning point low.

✪ In November 2020, heliocentric Saturn and Jupiter again made their 0-degree conjunction right at the time of the US Presidential election. But the market had already recorded a significant low point several months beforehand—in late March when the two planets were 12-degrees apart. This particular turning point will long be remembered as the COVID panic selloff.

☼ The next Saturn-Jupiter conjunction event will occur in 2038.

60-Year Spans of Time

Triple recurrences of the Gann Master Cycle can have a repetitive impact on geopolitics and on the financial markets. For example, *heliocentric* Jupiter and Saturn were conjunct in April 1961 in the latter part of the sign of Capricorn. The 1981 conjunction occurred in the sign of Libra. The June 2000 conjunction occurred in the sign of Taurus. The November 2020 conjunction occurred at 0-degrees Aquarius, a mere 7-degrees from where the 1961 conjunction had occurred. This seems to imply that after a 60-year time span, history could start to rhyme again. Consider the following examples of 60-year recurrences.

☼ The US equity market recorded its post-1929 crash low in 1932. Forward 60 years, and 1982 marked the start of what would be a major bull market.

☼ The year 1937 marked an interim peak on the US stock market. Forward 60 years, and an interim peak followed by the 1997 Asian currency crisis comes into focus.

☼ A low was recorded on the market in 1942. Forward 60 years to 2002 and a similar event occurred.

☼ A low was again recorded in 1949. Forward 60 years, and the March 2009 lows make an appearance.

☼ Late 1961 marked a turning point on the market. Add 60 years, and late 2021 likewise presented a turning point.

☼ From a low in 1962 the US market rallied briskly into 1965. This pattern seems to imply that 2023 to 2025 could see a positive tone to the equity market.

In the *Financial Astrology Almanac 2023*, I suggested that a firm market in 2023 seemed hard to fathom. Global tensions were spilling over, inflation was running hot, and recessionary fears were mounting. As I pen this manuscript in late October 2023, fears of an economic hard landing have abated and the S&P 500 has gained nearly 13% year to date. The 60-year recurrence theme seems to be holding true. **Barring some catastrophic geopolitical development (such as a spread of the Israel-Hamas conflict), the market appears likely to continue showing resilience in 2024.**

It is further interesting to note that the 60-year pattern can sometimes be seen outside of the financial markets. Consider that construction on the Pentagon building in Washington commenced on September 11, 1941. Sixty years later on September 11, 2001 the Pentagon was the target of the 9/11 terrorist attack.

The Summer of 1964 saw the Gulf of Tonkin event result in an acceleration of US military involvement in Vietnam. Add 60 years and ask the question—will 2024 see geopolitical events occurring that set the stage for wider-spread, multi-year global tensions? As I finish this manuscript in late October 2023, the Israel-Hamas conflict certainly has potential to spread throughout the Middle East.

The 18.6-Year Cycle

In addition to the Gann Master Cycle, there exists another long cycle that has a powerful impact on the financial markets (and the global real estate market as well).

This cycle was first written about in the 1930s by a mysterious figure called Louise McWhirter. [1] I say *mysterious* because in all my research I have neither come across any other writings by her nor have I found reference to her in other manuscripts. I am almost of the opinion that the name was a pseudonym for someone seeking to disseminate astrological ideas while remaining anonymous.

The Moon orbits the Earth in a plane of motion called the *lunar ecliptic.* Two planes that are not parallel will always intersect at two points. The two points where the lunar ecliptic intersects the plane of motion of planet Earth (the ecliptic plane) are termed the *North Node* and *South Node.* The two Nodes are opposite one another in the zodiac wheel. (Common practice among practitioners of astrology is to focus only on the North Node.)

McWhirter recognized that the transit of the North Node of the Moon around the zodiac wheel takes 18.6 years and that the Node progresses in a backwards (retrograde) motion through the zodiac signs.

Through examination of copious amounts of economic data provided by Leonard P. Ayers of the Cleveland Trust Company, McWhirter was able to conclude that when the North Node moves through certain zodiac signs, the economic business cycle reaches a low point. When the Node is passing certain other signs, the business cycle is at its strongest.

This line of thinking is still with us today. A notable authority embracing this economic cycle is British economist Fred Harrison. In his published works, he discusses this long economic cycle going back to the Industrial Revolution in the 1700s. But to maintain respect in academia, he stops just shy of stating a connection to the zodiac and the North Node. Two of his notable publications are *Power in the Land* and *Boom Bust 2010.*

McWhirter was able to discern the following from the Cleveland Trust data:

☼ As the Node enters Aquarius, the low point of economic activity is reached

- ✿ As the Node leaves Aquarius and begins to transit through Capricorn and Sagittarius, the economy starts to return to normal

- ✿ As the Node passes through Scorpio and Libra, the economy is functioning above normal

- ✿ As the Node transits through Leo, the high point in economic activity is reached

- ✿ As the Node transits through Cancer and Gemini, the economy is easing back towards normal

- ✿ As the Node enters the sign of Taurus, the economy begins to slow

- ✿ As the Node enters Aquarius, the low point of economic activity is reached and a full 18.6-year cycle is completed.

McWhirter further observed some secondary factors that could influence the tenor of economic activity in a *good* way, regardless of which sign the Node was in at the time:

- ✿ Jupiter being 0-degrees conjunct to the Node

- ✿ Jupiter being in Gemini or Cancer

- ✿ Pluto being at a favorable aspect to the Node.

McWhirter also observed some secondary factors that can influence the tenor of economic activity in a *bad* way, regardless of which sign the Node was in at the time:

- ✿ Saturn being 0, 90, or 180-degrees to the Node

- ✿ Saturn in Gemini or Cancer

- ✿ Uranus in Gemini

- ✿ Uranus being 0, 90 or 180-degrees to the Node

- ✿ Pluto being at an unfavorable aspect to the Node.

In early 2020, the North Node was in the sign of Cancer. The economy was gently easing, in alignment with McWhirter's predictions. None of the above mentioned secondary bad factors were in play. The COVID pandemic was met head-on with massive government stimulus to prevent a full-blown economic crisis.

The Node entered Taurus in early 2022 and the economy started to encounter stiff headwinds. These headwinds were emboldened by strained post-COVID supply chains, rising inflation, a flattening yield curve, and a Russian invasion of Ukraine. Market strategists soon started talking about recession.

Starting in late March 2022, Saturn formed a hard, 90-degree square aspect to the Node. In alignment with McWhirter's findings, this 90-degree square event negatively impacted the already slowing economy. Waves of selling pressure across equity markets lasted into late June 2022. Saturn turned retrograde on June 4, 2022. As it did, the reins of power were handed off to Uranus which then started its march towards a conjunction with the Node. The exact conjunction of Uranus to Node occurred on July 30. Once this exact conjunction was complete, Uranus and Node slowly drifted apart, maintaining a 3-to-4-degree unfavorable separation which still qualified as a conjunction. The negative tenor from this conjunction created another wave of weakness on equity markets that persisted into October 2022.

In late 2022 when I penned the 2023 Almanac manuscript, the Node was at 13 degrees of Taurus and was poised to enter Aries in mid-2023. Pluto would form an unfavorable, hard, square aspect to the Node in April 2023.

I suggested this Pluto square aspect would stimulate talk of economic weakness among the financial media. I further noted that in May 2023, Jupiter would form a conjunction to the Node, possibly allaying fears of a recession. By 2023 year-end, Pluto would be moving away from its conjunction with the Node, erasing any fears of recession. As I complete the final edits on this manuscript in late October 2023, I note that talk of recession by analysts and the financial media has abated. The naysayers who were forecasting a hard landing and a recession in 2023 have pushed their ideas off into late 2024.

What the naysayers do not realize is that for 2024, there will be no unfavorable aspects of Saturn or Pluto to the Node. This is good news. In addition, in May 2024, Jupiter will enter the sign of Gemini. McWhirter says Jupiter in Gemini will lend a positive tenor to the economy. Jupiter will persist in Gemini until mid-2025. This observation aligns with the suggestion offered earlier in this chapter of resilient markets into 2025. The Node will however enter the sign of Pisces in early 2025–a reminder that the 18.6-year cycle is getting long in the tooth, so to speak.

By mid-2026, the Node will be in Aquarius to mark the end of the 18.6-year cycle. I will not be surprised to see another financial crisis in late 2026 and into 2027.

There is one more cyclical event that troubles me. I hate to think about it, but it bears discussion. In 2026, Uranus will be in Gemini and also at a hard 90-degrees to the Node. This astro positioning warns of a negative economic time. It also warns of possible war. The 1776 natal horoscope for the USA has Uranus in the sign of Gemini. By mid-2027 Uranus will be exactly conjunct to the 1776 Uranus natal position at 8 degrees of Gemini. Uranus takes 84 years to travel one time through the zodiac. Subtract Uranus cycles from the year 2027 and past dates aligning to World War II, the US Civil War, and the War of Independence all come into focus. One need not look too hard to see how fragile the global geopolitical situation is. The seeds for a 2027 catastrophe may already have been sown, as the October 2023 events involving Israel, Gaza, and Iranian-backed terrorist groups have illustrated.

To sum up,

- ✿ The McWhirter 18.6-year cycle suggests the economy is on a slowing trajectory with Node in Aries. A full-blown financial crisis will manifest in late 2026 – early 2027

- ✿ For 2024, the economy will remain generally resilient

- ✿ In May 2024, Jupiter will enter the sign of Gemini. This should lend a favorable tone to the economy. Jupiter will remain in Gemini until mid-2025.

CHAPTER FOUR

Medium Cycles

Professor Weston's Cycles

In 1921, a mysterious person from Washington, D.C. using the name Professor Weston wrote a paper in which he analyzed decades of past price data for the Dow Jones Average. Who exactly Weston was, will likely never be known; another one of those figures who emerged to write his ideas down before vanishing into the ether.

His work was based on the premise that the Dow Jones price data was comprised of a series of interwoven, overlapping cycles. He applied cosine Fourier mathematics to the data to delineate the cycles. His analysis identified a 10-month, 14-month, 20-month and 28-month cycle pattern. Using the OPTUMA software, I have been able to demonstrate that these 10, 14, 20, and 28-month cycle intervals are indeed still evident today on a monthly chart of the Dow Jones Average.

Perhaps Weston knew W.D. Gann personally. Perhaps he just knew of him. In any case, Weston followed the 20-year Gann Master Cycle of Jupiter and Saturn.

Weston further broke this long cycle into two components of 10 years each.

His Fourier mathematical analysis showed that investors can expect:

- ☼ a 20-month market cycle to begin in November of the 1st year of the 10-year cycle

- ☼ another 20-month cycle to begin in November of the 5th year of the 10-year cycle

- ☼ 28-month cycles to begin in July of the 3rd and 7th years of the 10-year cycle

- ☼ a 10-month cycle to begin in November of the 9th year of the 10- year cycle

- ☼ a 14-month cycle to begin in September of the 10th year of the 10-year cycle.

To put this into perspective, a new Gann Master Cycle began on November 1, 2020 as heliocentric Jupiter and Saturn made a 0-degree aspect. The entire cycle will run until November 2040.

Following Weston's methodology for the first half of the overall Master Cycle (2020 to 2031):

- ☼ the first 20-month cycle will start in November 2020 and go to until July 2022

- ☼ a 28-month cycle will run from July 2023 through November 2025

- ☼ a 20-month cycle will run from November 2025 through July 2027

☼ a 28-month cycle will run July 2027 through November 2029

☼ a 10-month cycle will then run from November 2029 through September 2030

☼ lastly, a 14-month cycle will last until November 2031.

Looking at a chart of the S&P 500, one can delineate a cycle than runs from the lows of November 2020 to the lows of late June 2022.

We are now in the 28-month cycle that will terminate at or near November 2025.

Weston also postulated that in the various years of a 10-year segment of the overall Master Cycle, there would be market maxima as listed in Figure 4-1.

YEAR OF CYCLE	MAXIMA	MAXIMA
1	March	October
2		May
3	January	September
4	April	November
5	May	November
6		June
7	January	September
8		June
9	April	
10	February	August

Figure 4-1
Weston's Secondary Cycles

Weston calculated these events using cycles of Venus. He argued that the 16th harmonic of a 10-year period (120 months) was actually the heliocentric time it takes for Venus to orbit the Sun (120 x 30 / 16 = 225 days). Back-testing has shown that these dates should be taken with a time span of perhaps +/- 3 weeks. In other words, an October high might manifest in late September or perhaps in early-November.

Within the new Master Cycle that began in November 2020, Weston's work cautions investors to be alert for market maxima:

- ✷ in March 2021 and in October 2021
- ✷ in May 2022
- ✷ in January and September 2023
- ✷ in April and November 2024.

The S&P 500 recorded an interim high in late February 2021. By early March, the S&P had fallen over 200 points. A swing low was realized on March 4, 2021. An interim high maxima point was seen in September 2021, but the end of September recorded an interim low.

The S&P 500 registered an interim swing high on June 1, 2022, falling 500 points in the ensuing two weeks.

The S&P 500 registered a swing high on February 1, 2023 and proceeded to fall 400 points.

As I pen this manuscript in late October 2023, I note that the S&P 500 recorded a swing high in mid-August 2023 in keeping with Weston's prognostications. The trend change shaved 400 points of the index. The next maxima point will occur in April 2024.

April and November 2024 are forecast to again deliver market maxima points as per Weston's work.

Shemitah Years

Just as intriguing as Weston's cycles are medium-term cycles steeped in religious doctrine that intersect with financial market turning points. One religious concept is that of *Shemitah* which is rooted in the Hebrew Bible.

I first learned of Shemitah from the writings of Rabbi Jonathan Cahn. (1)(2)(3) On the surface, Cahn appears to be an average, ordinary Rabbi from New Jersey, USA. But behind the scenes, he has done a masterful job of applying Shemitah to the financial markets. His books include: *The Harbinger, The Book of Mysteries*, and *The Paradigm*.

As Cahn explains:

In the book of Exodus (Chapter 23, verses 10-11), it is written: *You may plant your land for six years and gather its crops. But during the seventh year, you must leave it alone and withdraw from it.*

In the book of Leviticus (Chapter 25, verses 20-22), it is written: *And if ye shall say: "What shall we eat the seventh year? Behold, we may not sow, nor gather in our increase"; then I will command My blessing upon you in the sixth year, and it shall bring forth produce for the three years. And ye shall sow the eighth year, and eat of the produce, the old store; until the ninth year, until the produce come in, ye shall eat the old store.*

Breaking these Biblical statements down into simple-to-understand terms means that every 7ᵗʰ year something will happen in the geopolitical sphere and on the financial markets.

The first Shemitah year in the modern State of Israel was 1951-52. Subsequent Shemitah years have been 1958–59, 1965–66, 1972–73,

1979–80, 1986–87, 1993–94, 2000–01, 2007–08, 2014-15, and 2021-2022. The next Shemitah year will be 2028-2029.

Shemitah years can be grinding and difficult for market participants. The most recent Shemitah year concluded in September 2022. During this Shemitah year, Russia invaded Ukraine; the price of crude oil surged; the price of gasoline at the pump rose smartly; fertilizer prices for farm operators jumped, food prices inflated; inflation reached the 8% level; the Federal Reserve ceased its liquidity injections into the financial system; BitCoin got pummeled, and the equity markets sagged from January through September.

A Shemitah year starts in the month of Tishrei (the first month of the Jewish civil calendar) and ends in the month of Elul. This timeframe on the Gregorian calendar will roughly run from September to the following September. The website **www.chabad.org** will help identify the exact dates.

The chart in Figure 4-2 illustrates the E-mini S&P 500 with some recent Shemitah years overlaid.

The time immediately following the conclusion of a Shemitah year has the potential to bring further drama. Equity markets can move modestly lower in the aftermath of a Shemitah year. The earlier-cited Biblical passages advise "… *ye shall sow the eighth year, and eat of the produce, the old store; until the ninth year, until the produce come in, ye shall eat the old store.*" In other words, do not expect a bounty in the year immediately after a Shemitah year.

As Figure 4-2 illustrates, some Shemitah years do minimal damage to the equity markets. This was the case for the 2014-2015 occurrence. However, during this Shemitah occurrence, Oil prices tumbled nearly $50 per barrel.

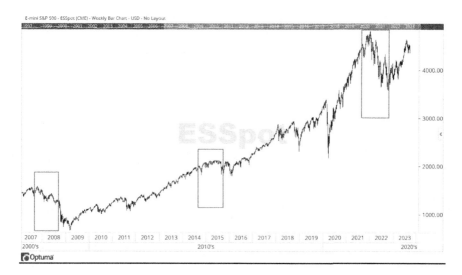

Figure 4-2
E-mini S&P 500 futures and Shemitah years

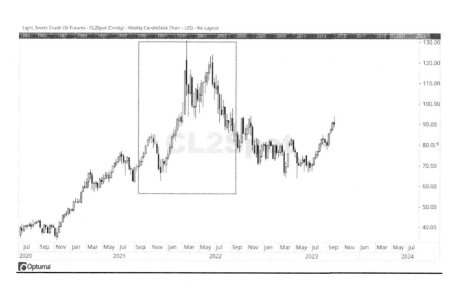

Figure 4-3
WTI Crude Oil futures and the 2021 Shemitah year

Some Shemitah years offer widespread damage. The 2021-2022 Shemitah year hit not only the equity market, but also the Oil market and the Bond market.

Figure 4-3 illustrates what happened to Oil prices during the 2021-2022 Shemitah year. Figure 4-4 illustrates the fall in Treasury Note prices (rise in interest rates) during the 2021-2022 Shemitah year.

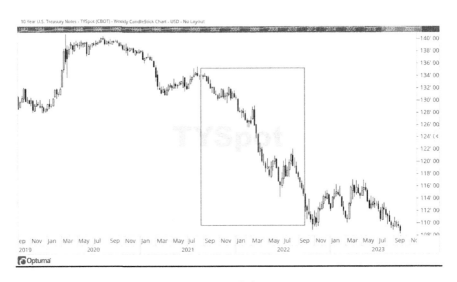

Figure 4-4
10-Year Treasury Note futures and the 2021 Shemitah year

Sacred Dates and Kabbalah Intervals

According to Rabbi Cahn, in addition to the Shemitah year, there are certain annual dates from the Hebrew calendar that can have a strong propensity to align with swing highs and lows on the New York Stock Exchange. While these dates actually comprise shorter-term cycles, I will discuss them in this chapter while still on the topic of Rabbi Cahn. He advises to pay close attention to six particular dates from the Hebrew calendar:

- ○ The 1st day of the month of Tishrei marks the start of the Jewish civil calendar, much like January 1 marks the start of the Gregorian calendar.

- ○ The 1st day of the month of Nissan marks the start of the Jewish sacred year.

- ○ The 3rd important date is the 9th day of the month of Tammuz which marks the date when Babylon destroyed the Temple at Jerusalem in 586 BC.

- ○ The 4th date is the 9th day of Av. Calamitous events have beset the Jewish people on the 9th of Av throughout history. In particular, Cahn tells of the mass expulsion of Jewish people from Spain in 1492. As this expulsion was going on, a certain explorer with three ships was about to set sail on a voyage of discovery. That explorer sailed out of port on August 3, 1492 which was one day after the 9th of Av. That explorer was Christopher Columbus.

- ○ The 5th key date in the Jewish calendar is Shemini Atzeret (the Gathering of the Eighth Day). This date typically falls somewhere in late September through late October in the month of Tishrei. It follows the 7-day Sukkot celebratory period and marks a time of bonding with God.

- ○ The 6th key date is Yom Kippur which falls on the 10th day of Tishrei. On the Gregorian calendar, this event lands in late September or early October.

The website **www.chabad.org** allows one to quickly scan back over a number of years to pick off these important dates. My back-testing has shown a correlation between equity market performance and these dates. The correlation is valid enough that I recommend traders and investors pay attention to these dates.

For 2023, these critical dates fell as follows: 1st of Nissan on March 23, the 9th of Tammuz on June 28, the 9th of Av on July 27, the 1st of Tishrei on September 16, 10th of Tishrei on September 25, and Shemini Atzeret on October 7.

The March 23 date was immediately preceded by a 400-point drawdown on the S&P 500. The 9th of Tammuz marked the end of a 100-point drawdown on the S&P 500 and the resumption of a rally. The 9th of Av date came a few days ahead of a swing high and a 6% drawdown on the S&P 500. The 1st of Tishrei marked an interim swing high and a failure of the S&P 500 to climb above its 50-day average. The 10th of Tishrei was immediately preceded by a stiff 1.6% drawdown on the S&P 500. The Shemini Atzeret date of October 7 marked a swing low and a 150-point rally on the S&P 500. This rally lost momentum when the news broke that Israel had been attacked by extremists from Gaza.

For 2024, these critical dates will fall as follows:

- ✡ **1st of Nissan on April 9**
- ✡ **9th of Tammuz on July 15**
- ✡ **9th of Av on August 13**
- ✡ **1st of Tishrei on October 3**
- ✡ **10th of Tishrei on October 12**
- ✡ **Shemini Atzeret from October 23-25.**

In addition to cycles related to religious doctrine, cycles related to Kabbalah mathematics are also intriguing. A 2005 article in *Trader's World* magazine (4) suggested that W.D. Gann might have been given knowledge of Jewish mysticism based on Kabbalah doctrine. Gann apparently had connections to a New York personality named Sepharial who is said to have taught Gann about astrology and esoteric matters.

The Kabbalah centers around the Hebrew Alef-bet (alphabet). The Hebrew Alef-bet comprises 22 letters. In Kabbalistic methodology, these letters are assigned a numerical value. Starting with the first letter, values are 1, 2, 3, 4, 5, 6, 7, 8, 9, 10, 20, 30, 40, 50, 60, 70, 80, 90, 100, 200, 300, and 400.

There are many mathematical techniques that can be applied to parsing the Alef-bet. One in particular involves taking the odd-numbered letters and the even numbered letters and assigning their appropriate numerical values.

The numerical value (sum total) of the Alef-bet is 1495. The sum total of the odd-numbered letters is 625. The sum total of the even numbered letters is 870.

- ✿ 625/1495 = 42%. Taking a circle of 360-degrees, 42% is 150.5 degrees.

- ✿ 870/1495 = 58%. Taking a circle of 360-degrees, 58% is 209.5 degrees.

- ✿ Kabbalists are also well aware of phi as it pertains to the Golden Mean. Phi is famously known as 1.618.

- ✿ 1/phi = 61.8%. Taking a circle of 360-degrees, 61.8% is 222.5 degrees.

- ✿ 1 – (1/phi) = 38.2%. Taking a circle of 360-degrees, 38.2% is 137.5 degrees.

From a significant price low (or high) starting point, one can examine price charts for time intervals when a heliocentric planet advances 137.5, 150.5, 209.5, or 222.5-degree amounts. My back-testing has shown that Venus and Mars heliocentric advances are very apt to align to market turning points.

To illustrate, consider the significant low in March 2009 on the S&P 500 as a start point. Applying the above described 137.5-degree ratio, what emerges is the discovery that 11 years after the March 2009 lows, one of the Venus 137.5-degree advancements of heliocentric Venus landed on the March 2020 lows.

Extending these various degree intervals forward from the March 2009 lows reveals many correlations to swing points on the S&P 500 chart. For example, Figure 4-5 shows how a 137.5-degree heliocentric Venus interval landed near the October 2022 market low. Also shown in Figure 4-5 as a dashed line is a 209.5-degree heliocentric Venus interval that landed at the October 2022 market low. Two Venus heliocentric intervals landing within days of each other is a powerful occurrence.

Although not shown in Figure 4-5, a Mars 150.5-degree heliocentric interval extended from the December 2021 market swing high point landed right at the September 2022 counter-trend reversal point that culminated in the October 2022 low.

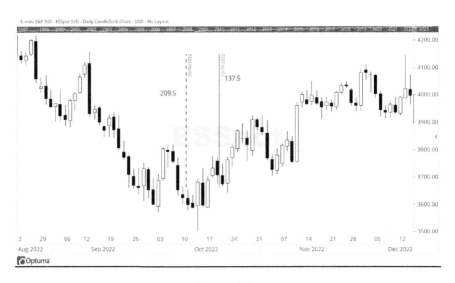

Figure 4-5
E-mini S&P 500 and Venus heliocentric degree intervals

To further illustrate the effect of these intervals, consider that in November 2008 the Nasdaq recorded a low that was slightly less than the March 2009 low. Using this November 2008 date as a start point and applying 137.5-degree, 150.5-degree, and 209.5-degree Venus-intervals shows correlations still exist in 2023 as illustrated in Figure 4-6.

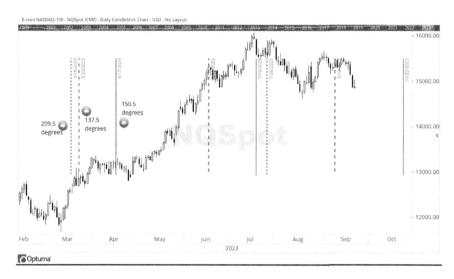

Figure 4-6
Nasdaq and Venus heliocentric degree intervals

Application of Venus and Mars intervals is not limited to equity markets. These intervals can be applied to commodity price charts too. Figure 4-7 illustrates the application of 137.5, 150.5, and 209.5-degree intervals of heliocentric Mars from the 2011 swing high point on Gold futures.

The Gold price swing low in March 2023 aligns to a Mars 137.5-degree interval. A swing pivot point in July aligns to a 150.5-degree interval. The swing high in early May aligns to 222.5-degree interval. Late December 2023 will bring another 137.5-degree interval.

Although not shown on Figure 4-7, projecting Venus 137.5-degree intervals from March 2020, reveals an interval that landed five days prior to the 2023 terrorist attacks in Israel. News of the attack sent Gold prices surging.

However, October 28, 2023 saw the price of Gold stop rising. This price point marked a Fibonacci 78.6% retracement of the overall price decline from May 2023 to October 2023. After failing to penetrate the 78.6% retracement level, price retreated 38.2% of the October rally and then attempted to rally again. This rally attempt was successful and as I finish the edits on this manuscript in early December 2023, Gold price looks set to challenge the May 2023 highs.

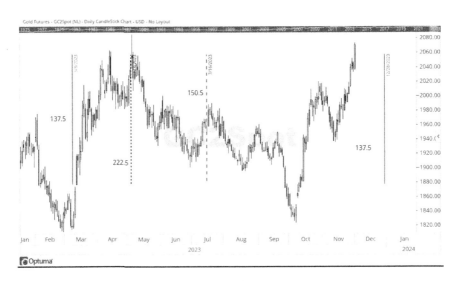

Figure 4-7
Gold price and Mars heliocentric intervals

Consider also the 2008 significant price high on WTI Oil futures. Extending Mars 150.5-degree intervals from those highs reveals that an interval landed several days after the steep price decline that briefly took Oil prices negative in 2020. A 137.5-degree interval landed mere days after the March 2022 price highs at $130 per barrel. In 2023, a swing low at $67 per barrel in June aligned to a Mars 150.5-degree interval. November 8, 2023 will see a 209.5-degree interval manifest.

Consider too, the Soybean market. From a significant price low in 2019, heliocentric Mars intervals of 137.5, 150.5, and 209.5-degrees can be seen aligning to various swing highs and lows.

To assist you in identifying some *heliocentric* intervals in 2024:

- ☼ **For the S&P 500 in 2024 (using a start point of March 2009), the 137.5-degree intervals of Venus will occur: March 17, June 10, September 3, and November 28.**

- ☼ **For the S&P 500 in 2024 (using a start point of March 2009), the 150.5-degree intervals of Venus will occur: February 3, May 7, August 8, and November 10.**

- ☼ **For the S&P 500 in 2024 (using a start point of March 2009), the 209.5-degree intervals of Venus will occur: March 18, July 27, and December 5.**

- ☼ **For the S&P 500 in 2024 (using a start point of March 2009), the 222.5-degree intervals of Venus will occur: January 1, April 30, and September 15,**

- ☼ **For the Nasdaq in 2024 (using a start point of the November 2008 lows), the 137.5-degree intervals of Venus will occur: February 27, May 24, August 16, and November 10.**

- ☼ **For the Nasdaq in 2024 (using a start point of the November 2008 lows), the 150.5-degree intervals of Venus will occur: January 22, April 25, July 27, and October 29.**

- ☼ **For the Nasdaq in 2024 (using a start point of the November 2008 lows), the 209.5-degree intervals of Venus will occur: April 14, August 22, and December 31.**

- ☼ For Oil in 2024 (using a start point of July 14, 2008), the 137.5-degree interval of Mars will occur: April 30, and December 21.

- ☼ For Oil in 2024 (using a start point of July 14, 2008), the 150.5-degree interval of Mars will occur: March 31, and December 17.

- ☼ For Oil in 2024 (using a start point of July 14, 2008), the 209.5-degree interval of Mars will occur: July 20.

- ☼ For Oil in 2024 (using a start point of July 14, 2008), the 222.5-degree interval of Mars will occur: September 22.

- ☼ For Gold in 2023 (using a start point of September 6, 2011), the Mars degree intervals will occur: April 22 (150.5-degrees), June 23 (137.5), and October 25 (209.5).

- ☼ For Soybeans in 2023 (using a start point of May 13, 2019), the Mars degree intervals will occur: February 25, and November 4 (150.5), May 29 (137.5), October 24 (209.5), and February 3 (222.5).

- ☼ For the US Dollar Index in 2023 (using a start point of 21 April 2008), the Mars degree intervals will occur: February 1 and October 6 (150.5-degrees), September 6 (209.5-degrees), February 26 and October 10 (137.5-degrees), and July 16 (222.5-degrees).

- ☼ For the US Dollar Index in 2023 (using a start point of 21 April 2008), the Venus 137.5-degree intervals will occur: January 18, April 13, July 8, and October 1. The 150-degree intervals will occur: April 3, July 6, September 18, and December 3. A 209.5-degree interval will land September 2 and a 222.5-degree interval will land on November 19.

Beyond these examples, for a particular market index, currency, or commodity, identify a key high or low point. With heliocentric data in hand, count forward the requisite number of degrees (137.5, 150.5,

209.5 or 222.5) and see where the next intervals manifest. Not every single interval will necessarily align to a significant price inflection point. However, the correlation between these degree intervals and inflection points is robust enough that they cannot be ignored.

CHAPTER FIVE
Shorter Cycles

Venus Cosmic Events

Cycles of Venus play a key role in forecasting trend changes on financial markets.

Venus orbits the Sun in 225 days relative to an observer standing at a fixed venue like the Sun. This is its *heliocentric* orbital time.

To an observer situated on Earth (a moving frame of reference), Venus appears to take 584 days to orbit the Sun. This is its *geocentric* orbital time.

During this 584-day geocentric orbital period, there will be periods of time when Venus is situated between Earth and Sun. This is its *inferior conjunction*. As Venus slowly moves out of this conjunction, it will become visible in the early morning hours as the *Morning Star*.

During its 584-day geocentric orbital period, there will be periods of time when the Sun is situated between Venus and Earth. This is its *superior conjunction*. As it moves out of this conjunction, it becomes visible in the evening before sunset as the *Evening Star*.

When one considers the pattern of superior and inferior conjunctions over time, the influence of Venus becomes even more intriguing. Multiplying the 584-day geocentric cycle by 5 yields a value of 2920. Dividing 2920 by the 365-day orbital period of Earth yields a value of 8. The ratio of the Venus geocentric orbital period to the orbital period of Earth is thus a 5:8 ratio. Multiplying eight by five yields 40, a symbolic number cited frequently in Biblical texts. Dividing 5 by 8 gives 62.5% which is close to the Fibonacci ratio of 62.8%.

Venus influences the human psyche as it shifts from being visible in the morning to being visible in the evening and vice versa.

Venus was at superior conjunction on March 28 2013 (8 Aries), October 25, 2014 (1 Scorpio), June 6, 2016 (16 Gemini), January 8, 2018 (18 Capricorn), August 14, 2019 (27 Leo), March 26, 2021 (6 Aries), and October 22, 2022 (4 Libra).

Venus was at inferior conjunction on June 6, 2012 (15 Gemini), January 11, 2014 (21 Capricorn), August 15, 2015 (22 Leo), March 25, 2017 (4 Aries), October 26, 2018 (3 Scorpio), June 4, 2020 (13 Gemini), and January 9, 2022 (18 Capricorn), and August 13, 2023 (20 Leo).

Each of these superior and inferior dates aligns to a pivot swing point on a chart of the S&P 500. The magnitude of the price reaction following these pivot points varies. Nevertheless, these inferior and superior events deserve close scrutiny. I believe, that somehow, human emotion is hardwired to events of Venus.

- ☿ The inferior conjunction event on June 4, 2020 delivered a 200- point drop on the S&P 500. But the Federal Reserve came to the rescue with more fiat liquidity to save the markets from steeper decline.

- ☿ The superior conjunction event of March 26, 2021 was immediately preceded by the Dow Jones dropping 1100 points (high to low) over six trading sessions.

- ☿ The Venus inferior conjunction on January 9, 2022 confirmed that the trend had indeed changed on equity markets. The Federal Reserve vowed that it was intent on raising rates. Emotion on Wall Street boiled over.

- ☿ The Venus superior conjunction on October 22, 2022 came a handful of days after the critical low that spelled the end of the 2022 bear market. This timeframe also yielded chaos in the UK as newly minted Prime Minister Lizz Truss resigned.

- ☿ Venus was at inferior conjunction on August 13, 2023. The S&P 500 reached a swing high point on August 1. The inferior conjunction event intensified the weakness by hastening the price decline.

Venus will be at superior conjunction on June 4, 2024.

Furthermore, if one plots these groups of superior conjunction events on a zodiac wheel, it becomes evident that they can be joined to form a 5-pointed star called a pentagram. Likewise, the inferior conjunction degree points can also be plotted and when joined will form a pentagram. Such are the mysteries of our cosmos.

As Venus orbits around the Sun following the ecliptic plane, it moves above and below the plane. The high points and low points made during this travel are termed *declination maxima* and *minima*. Declination maxima and minima play key roles in price trend changes on financial markets. (Recall from an earlier chapter where it was noted that declination is a heliocentric phenomenon.) Many financial astrology software programs default to displaying declination as a geocentric phenomenon.

- ✪ The Venus declination minimum in early September, 2021 was followed by a 200-point drawdown on the S&P 500. A brief recovery attempt followed that lasted into early January 2022 but failed to hold as Venus marked Inferior Conjunction and maximum declination.

- ✪ Venus at declination minimum in late April 2022 marked the half-way point in a sizeable selloff that was part of the ongoing market weakness.

- ✪ Venus at declination maximum in mid-August 2022 marked the end of a counter-trend rally. From here, the S&P 500 would descend to its October low point and Superior Conjunction.

- ✪ Venus at declination minimum in early December 2022 marked the start of a 300-point retreat on the S&P 500.

- ✪ Venus at declination maximum in late March 2023 marked the general start of a rally that endured until August 2023. Emotion was so fixated on the market moving higher that the Venus declination minimum in July failed to interrupt the trend.

- ✪ November 6 2023 saw Venus at its declination maximum again.

Venus will be at its exact declination minimum on February 27 and October 9, 2024. Venus will be at its exact declination maximum on June 17, 2024.

Another cyclical event pertaining to Venus is its *retrograde* events. From our vantage point on Earth, we describe the position of Venus relative to one of the twelve star constellations in the sky. There will be one time (occasionally two times) time per year when Earth and Venus pass by each other. Owing to the different orbital speeds of Earth and Venus, as Venus laps past Earth, there will be a period of time when we see Venus in the previous constellation to where it was just prior to starting to pass by Earth. For example, we might start off seeing Venus against the star constellation of Gemini. As Venus begins to lap past Earth, we will see Venus against the star constellation of Taurus. As Venus passes by Earth, we will see Venus again in Taurus. Of course, Venus has not physically reversed course and moved backwards. This is an optical illusion created by the different orbital speeds of Venus and Earth.

These brief illusory periods of backwards motion are what astrologers call retrograde events. To ancient societies, retrograde events were of great significance as human emotion was often seen to be changeable at those times.

There is a curiously strong correlation between equity markets and Venus retrograde. Sometimes Venus retrograde events encompass a sharp market inflection point. Sometimes a market peak or bottom will follow closely behind a retrograde event. Sometimes a peak or bottom will immediately precede a retrograde event. I believe human emotion is hardwired to retrograde events of Venus. When a Venus retrograde event is approaching, use a suitable chart technical indicator to determine if the price trend is changing.

Figure 5-1 illustrates price behavior of the E-mini S&P 500 index in early August 2023 at the Venus retrograde event. The retrograde event marked a swing pivot high and a change of trend.

Knowing that the potential exists for sizeable moves, aggressive traders can avail themselves of these retrograde correlations. Less aggressive investors may simply wish to place a stop loss order under their positions to guard against sharp price pullbacks.

Figure 5-1
E-mini S&P 500 index and Venus retrograde

The influence of Venus also extends beyond just the equity markets. Commodities can also be influenced. Consider the price of Gold:

✿ In early 2022 just as the Venus retrograde event started, Gold prices started to trend higher, gaining over $200 per ounce.

✿ In August 2023, Venus was again retrograde. Two days before the retrograde event, Gold failed to maintain its momentum above the 50-day average. The trend changed to bearish and the price began to decline.

Consider too the price of Oil and the price of Wheat:

✿ As the Venus retrograde event started in early 2022, Oil prices started to trend higher, moving from $67 per barrel to $130 per barrel.

✿ The Venus retrograde event in August 2023 amounted to a trap for many Oil futures traders. Mid-way through the retrograde event, Oil prices started falling. After a $6 per barrel drawdown, Oil prices suddenly rebounded leaving short sellers scrambling to cover their positions.

✧ As the Venus retrograde event in early 2022 wrapped up, Wheat prices started to rally, moving from $7 per bushel to $13 per bushel.

✧ In August 2023, as Venus turned retrograde Wheat prices started to tumble. By the time the retrograde event was complete, Wheat prices had declined by $2 per bushel.

For 2024, traders and investors can rest easy. There will be no Venus retrograde events to contend with.

Mercury Cosmic Events

Mercury is the smallest planet in our solar system. It is also the closest planet to the Sun. As a result of its proximity to the powerful gravitational pull of the Sun, Mercury moves very quickly, completing one heliocentric cycle of the Sun in 88 days.

Mercury has an eccentric orbit in which its distance from the Sun will range from 46 million km to 70 million km. When Mercury is nearer to the Sun (46 million kms away), it is moving at its fastest (56.6 km per second). When Mercury is farther from the Sun (70 million km away), it is moving slower (38.7 km per second). [1]

When Mercury is at its closest orbital point to the Sun it is said to be at *perihelion*. When Mercury is at its farthest orbital point to the Sun it is said to be at *aphelion*. These cosmic occurrences seem to affect human emotion and in turn the financial markets.

For example, in 2020, Mercury was at perihelion just as the equity markets were reaching a peak ahead of the COVID panic selloff. Emotions were stoked and investors went into full panic mode at the thought of a respiratory virus sweeping the globe. The selloff lows came in late March just as Mercury was nearing aphelion. This event seemed to calm fears.

Mercury perihelion and aphelion events do not always seamlessly correlate to all market inflection points. Nevertheless, past market performance suggests these dates should be anticipated by traders and investors.

For 2023, Mercury was at perihelion at: January 2, March 31, June 27, September 23, and December 21. Aphelion dates were: February 15, May 14, August 10, and November 7.

The January 2 perihelion event aligned to a swing bottom on the S&P 500. March 31 marked the end of a rally and the start of a sideways consolidation. June 27 saw some minor volatility, but emotions were firmly bullish and investors did not get flustered. The September 23 event aligned to a sudden 1.6% selloff on the S&P 500 index.

The February 15 aphelion event marked a swing pivot high. The May 14 event started a renewed rally after a period of consolidation. The August 10 event intensified what was already a weak market.

For 2024:

☼ **Mercury will be at perihelion: March 17, June 13, September 9, and December 6.**

☼ **Mercury will be at aphelion: February 2, April 30, July 27, and October 23.**

Related to Mercury's orbit is its *elongation*. As discussed earlier in Chapter One, elongation refers to the angle between a planet and the Sun, using Earth as a reference point. Figure 5-2 illustrates the concept of elongation. Times when Mercury is at its greatest elongations bear a strong correlation to short-term turning points on financial markets.

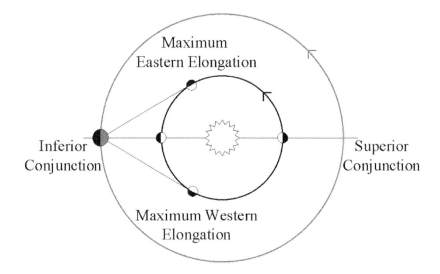

Figure 5-2
Elongation of Mercury

In 2023:

- ☼ Mercury was at its greatest easterly elongation April 11, August 10, and December 4

- ☼ Mercury was at its greatest westerly elongation January 30, May 29, and September 22.

Figure 5-3 illustrates some of these 2023 events overlaid on a chart of the E-mini S&P 500.

A swing high in February was preceded by a westerly elongation event. A sideways consolidation pattern in April and May was bracketed by an easterly and westerly elongation event. The market peaked in early August, several days prior to an easterly elongation event. A westerly event in September marked the end of a stiff drawdown in price of the S&P 500 index.

Figure 5-3
2023 Mercury Elongation Events

☼ **For 2024, Mercury will be at its greatest easterly elongation March 24, July 22, and November 16.**

☼ **For 2024, Mercury will be at its greatest westerly elongation January 12, May 9, September 4, and December 24.**

In addition to elongation events, there will be retrograde events. Mercury retrograde has been popularized by classical astrologers who tell people not to sign important contracts during Mercury retrograde, not to cross the street, not to leave their houses and so on. While I tend to ignore this mundane talk, I have noticed a striking correlation between financial market behavior and Mercury retrograde events.

There will be three (occasionally four) times during a year when Earth and Mercury pass by each other. Owing to the different orbital speeds of Earth and Mercury, as Mercury starts to lap past Earth there will be a period of time when we see Mercury in what appears to be the previous constellation. For example, just as Mercury starts to lap past Earth, we might start off seeing Mercury against the star constellation of Gemini. As Mercury continues to lap past Earth, we will see Mercury against the star constellation of Taurus. As Mercury finally passes by Earth, we will see Mercury again in Taurus. Of course, Mercury has not physically reversed course and moved backwards. This is an optical illusion created by the different orbital speeds of Mercury and Earth.

To ancient societies, retrograde events were of great significance as human emotion was often seen to be changeable at these events. I further believe that human emotion is hardwired to retrograde events of Mercury as these events often align to short term price trend changes. Are these trend changes caused by emotional discomfort that compels us to buy or sell stocks and commodity futures contracts?

Sometimes Mercury retrograde events encompass a sharp market inflection point. Sometimes a market peak or bottom will follow closely behind a retrograde event; sometimes a peak or bottom will immediately precede a retrograde event. Mercury retrograde events can be highly unpredictable as to when the impact on a financial instrument will appear.

Knowing that a Mercury retrograde event is approaching, traders and investors should remain alert for indications of a trend change using chart technical indicators.

Figure 5-4 illustrates three Mercury retrograde events from 2023 overlaid on a chart of the E-mini S&P 500. The chart has been fitted with the True Strength indicator. Note how this indicator provides crossovers that denote trend changes at the retrograde events.

What emerged from the January 2023 retrograde event was a trend change and a rally. The April-May event saw the True Strength Index cross negative as price lapsed into a sideways pattern. The retrograde event that started in late August started a counter-trend rally. No sooner was retrograde complete than the downward bearish trend resumed.

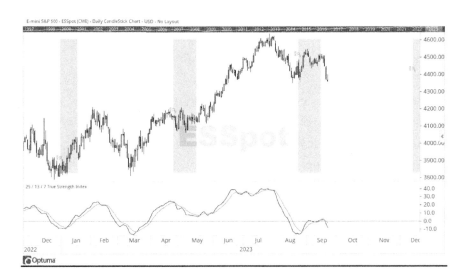

Figure 5-4
E-mini S&P 500 and Mercury retrograde

Mercury retrograde events can sometimes be seen influencing commodity markets. For example, Figure 5-5 illustrates a Wheat futures price chart overlaid with Mercury retrograde events from 2023. In early January, no sooner was retrograde complete than a rally commenced. The retrograde event in April-May was characterized by a sharp counter-trend rally. The retrograde event in August-September saw Wheat prices trying to form a bottom amidst significant volatility.

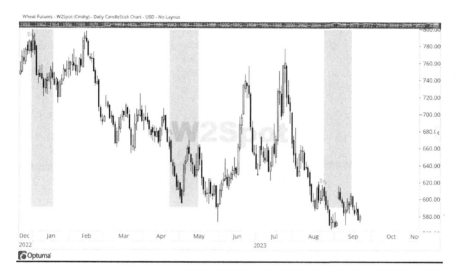

Figure 5-5
Mercury retrograde and Wheat futures

For 2024, Mercury will be:

☿ **retrograde from April 1 through April 24**

☿ **retrograde from August 5 through August 27**

☿ **retrograde from November 26 through December 14.**

Pleiades Aspects

Another short-term phenomenon involves the *Pleiades*–a cluster of stars situated in the constellation of Taurus. On the geocentric zodiac wheel, the position of 27 degrees Taurus aligns with the Pleiades star cluster.

The Pleiades are sometimes called the *Seven Sisters*. Many cultures from around the world have mythological tales that incorporate the Pleiades.

For example, the Cree indigenous people of western Canada regard the Pleiades as a hole in the sky from which they came. As the story goes, Sky Woman spotted Earth and expressed a desire to visit the planet. With help from Spider Woman, who spun a web, Sky Woman was able to complete her journey to planet Earth.

The following chart depicts daily price action on Gold futures. The chart has been overlaid with Venus and Sun transiting past the Pleiades at 27 Taurus between April 11 and May 17, 2023. These transits bracket the timeframe during which a top in Gold prices was observed near $2060 per ounce. This top has not been challenged as of mid-October, 2023.

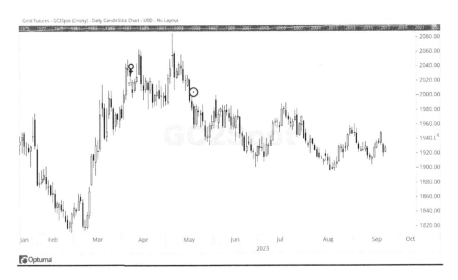

Figure 5-6
Gold Price and Transits of the Pleiades

In 2024:

- ☼ **Sun will pass the Pleiades point between May 14 and May 25**

- ☼ **Venus will pass the Pleiades point in Taurus between May 17 and May 27**

☼ **Mars will pass the Pleiades point between July 12 and July 24.**

Sirius Rising and Setting

Sirius is the brightest star in our night sky. This likely explains why ancient civilizations held it in such reverence. The Egyptians timed the planting of their crops to the rising of Sirius in the early morning sky. The ancient Romans held sacrificial ceremonies that coincided with the appearance of Sirius in the night sky. In ancient Persian mythology, Sirius is revered as the rain-maker divinity. This ancient reverence makes me wonder if humans are emotionally hard wired to the appearance of Sirius. For latitudes in North America, Sirius can be seen setting in the southwest evening sky in April and rising in the early morning sky in mid-August. Back-testing shows that markets can be prone to increased volatility in the April and August time frames.

Synodic Cycles

As discussed in an earlier chapter, planetary movements can be examined in terms of synodic cycles (geocentric) and sidereal cycles (heliocentric).

The time it takes from Venus recording a conjunction with Sun until that same conjunction occurs again is 584 days. Mars takes 780 days from a Sun/Mars conjunction to the next Sun/Mars conjunction. Sun/Saturn conjunctions are 376 days apart. Other outer planets take 367 to 399 days.

Synodic cycles involving celestial bodies such as Sun, Mercury, and Venus relative to slower moving bodies such as Pluto, Saturn, and Jupiter are of particular interest in identifying trend turning points on equity and commodity markets. A trailblazer in correlating this synodic behavior to the markets was the late American financial astrologer, Jeanne Long. [2]

As an example, Figure 5-7 illustrates Oil prices and the Sun-Pluto synodic cycle. The aspects overlaid on this chart are 0, 90, 120, and 180-degrees. All aspects have been drawn to within orb (+/-5 degrees of exact alignment). These aspects can be seen aligning to price pivot points.

Figure 5-7
Sun-Pluto aspects and Oil prices

Figure 5-8 illustrates Silver prices in the context of aspects between Venus and Jupiter. The aspects overlaid on this chart are 0, 90, and 120, degrees. All aspects have been drawn to within orb (+/-5 degrees of exact alignment). These aspects can be seen aligning to swing high and swing low pivot points.

Figure 5-9 illustrates aspects between Sun and Jupiter in the context of the S&P 500. The aspects overlaid on this chart are 0, 90, and 120 degrees. All aspects have been drawn to within orb (+/-5 degrees of exact alignment). These aspects can be seen aligning to swing high and swing low pivot points.

Figure 5-8
Venus-Jupiter aspects and Silver prices

Figure 5-9
Sun-Jupiter aspects and E-mini S&P 500

Figure 5-10 illustrates aspects between Mercury and Saturn during 2023 in the context of Soybean futures. A conjunction aspect in early

March triggered a $1.50 per bushel drawdown ($7500 per contract). A 120-degree trine event in late June aligned to a significant price spike. A 180-degree opposition event in late July triggered a drawdown of over $2 per bushel.

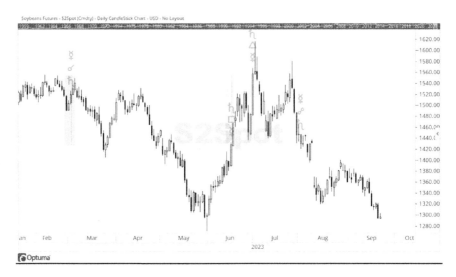

Figure 5-10
Mercury-Saturn aspects and Soybeans

Over and above Jeanne Long's excellent work from years ago, back-testing has shown that:

❖ heliocentric Jupiter-Neptune aspects influence trend changes on Wheat and Corn

❖ Mercury-Saturn aspects influence short term trend changes on Euro, British pound, Australian dollar, Canadian dollar currency futures, Corn futures, and meats futures (Live cattle, Feeder cattle, Lean hogs)

❖ Mercury-Jupiter aspects influence Wheat futures, 10-Year Treasury Notes, and 30-Year Bonds

❖ Sun-Neptune aspects influence Gold futures and Coffee futures

☼ Sun-Pluto aspects influence Copper, Cocoa, and Sugar futures

☼ Sun-Jupiter aspects influence the Nasdaq.

For 2024, the above-described aspects will occur on following dates:

PLANETARY PAIR	ASPECT	DATES
Sun-Pluto	0 degrees	January 12-28
	60 degrees	March 17-24
	90 degrees	April 16-27
	120 degrees	May 15-28
	180 degrees	July 15-28
	120 degrees	September 16-26
	60 degrees	November 16-25

PLANETARY PAIR	ASPECT	DATES
Sun-Jupiter	90 degrees	January 20-February 2
	60 degrees	February-March 4
	0 degrees	May 7-May 29
	60 degrees	August 7-August 11
	90 degrees	September 5-18
	120 degrees	October 6 -October 20
	180 degrees	December 1-December 13

PLANETARY PAIR	ASPECT	DATES
Sun-Neptune	60 degrees	January 11-18
	0 degrees	March 8-24
	60 degrees	May 15-May 22
	90 degrees	June 14-25
	120 degrees	July 15-28
	180 degrees	September 14-26
	120 degrees	November 12-24
	90 degrees	December 14-25

PLANETARY PAIR	ASPECT	DATES
Venus-Jupiter	120 degrees	January 22-February 3
	90 degrees	February 19-29
	60 degrees	March 21-March 26
	0 degrees	May 14-May 30
	60 degrees	July 18-July 24
	90 degrees	August 13-23
	120 degrees	September 8-20
	180 degrees	October 28-November 8
	120 degrees	December 14-24

PLANETARY PAIR	ASPECT	DATES
Mercury-Saturn	0 degrees	February 24-March 6
	60 degrees	April 3-7
	60 degrees	May 7-24
	60 degrees	November 29-December 4
	60 degrees	December 18-23
	90 degrees	June 11-18
	90 degrees	November 6-13
	120 degrees	June 26-July 2
	120 degrees	October 18-26
	180 degrees	July 27-August 6

PLANETARY PAIR	ASPECT	DATES
Mercury-Jupiter	60 degrees	January 14-20
	0 degrees	February 23-Mar 3
	60 degrees	May 25-May 29
	90 degrees	June 9-14
	120 degrees	June 23-29
	180 degrees	September 13-21
	120 degrees	October 17-26
	90 degrees	November 7-16
	90 degrees	December 2-11
	90 degrees	December 19-31

The Bradley Model

Planetary aspect cycles pre-date the work of Jeanne Long. In 1946, astrologer Donald Bradley[3] defined a model based on *geocentric* pairings of planets. In his model, as a pair of planets approach one another and come to within 15-degrees separation, a sinusoidal weighting is applied to the separation. At a 15-degree separation the weighting assigned is zero. At a 0-degree separation (planets are conjunct) the weighting is 10. Bradley's model also included a variable defined as the mathematical average of the declination of Venus and Mars. Running the model on a daily basis generates a plot with many inflection points. The image in Figure 5-11 illustrates the Bradley Model plot for 2024.

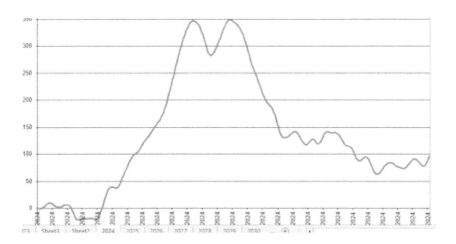

Figure 5-11
Bradley Model Plot

Many people mis-interpret the Bradley Model. They take the slope of the model to mean the S&P 500 price trend will have the same slope. That is—they feel the market should rise when the Bradley plot is sloping higher. I have come to realize that the most effective way to interpret the model is to focus on the inflection points in the output plot.

An inflection point, when the slope of the plot suddenly changes, has a very strong correlation to price changes on the S&P 500. I take this as evidence that planetary pairings affect the human emotions of fear and greed, both of which propel financial markets.

For 2024, the following dates are the inflection points on the model plot:

- ☼ **January 12**
- ☼ **February 7, 26**
- ☼ **March 10, 15**
- ☼ **April 28**
- ☼ **May 26**
- ☼ **June 11, 29**
- ☼ **August 18, 28**
- ☼ **September 7, 13, 19, 28**
- ☼ **October 27**
- ☼ **November 2, 13, 24**
- ☼ **December 8, 18, 26.**

Note the alignment to Weston's work which calls for a maxima in April 2024 and a maxima in November 2024. The Bradley model has an inflection point around April 28 and a series of inflection points in November.

Lunar and Planetary Declination

The Moon's orbit around the Earth can be described in terms of either synodic or sidereal cycles. The sidereal period of the Moon is 27.5 days (as viewed from a fixed reference like the Sun) and the synodic period is

29.53 days (as viewed from our vantage point here on Earth). This latter period lends itself to the expression *lunar month*.

During each synodic lunar cycle, the Moon can be seen to vary in its position above and below the lunar ecliptic; it will go from maximum declination to maximum declination.

Moon declination takes on an intriguing aspect when one considers that in 2020 two of the Moon declination minima events occurred on February 19 and March 18. The exact trend change turning point ahead of the COVID panic sell-off came at February 19. The panic lows came at March 23, mere days after the declination low.

It is said that W.D. Gann was a proponent of following lunar declination when trading Soybeans and Cotton. It is likely that he appreciated how the Moon's gravitational pull governs the ocean tides. With our bodies being substantially water, he was likely postulating that the Moon was influencing the emotions of Soybean and Cotton traders.

Figure 5-12 presents a chart of Soybeans with the Moon declination in the lower panel. The vertical lines overlaid on the chart illustrate the propensity for declination maxima, minima, and zero points to align to price swings. (Not all declination points have been overlaid on the chart.) A 4-hour chart would be the ideal way to study these price swings closely.

In Mr. Gann's day, he had access to ticker tape data which allowed him to accurately study intraday price action on days when Moon was nearing its declination minima, maxima, and zero declination points.

Figure 5-12 helps one appreciate why a trader like W.D. Gann would have used lunar declination phenomenon to give himself an advantage in the Soybean market.

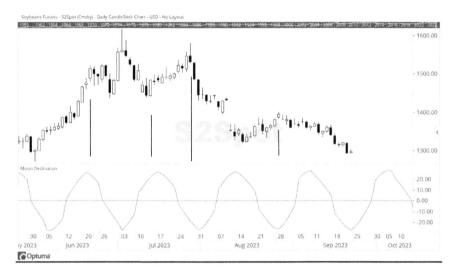

Figure 5-12
Moon Declination and Soybeans

Figure 5-13 illustrates Moon declination and Gold futures. Maximum, minimum, and zero levels of lunar declination bear a strong correlation to swing pivots in price. It is fascinating to note that the price of Gold exhibited a pivot swing point at a Moon maximum declination event in early October just as the terrorist events in Israel were launched. Gold price surged on October 13, 2023 as Moon was passing through zero-degrees of declination. This was also the date that the Israeli military announced it would be staging a ground attack into the Gaza region. The Moon, without doubt, affects human emotion and thereby the markets.

Moon declination events tend to align very closely to price swings on individual stocks. Consider the favorite stocks you enjoy trading in and out of. Does Moon declination align to periodic price swing points?

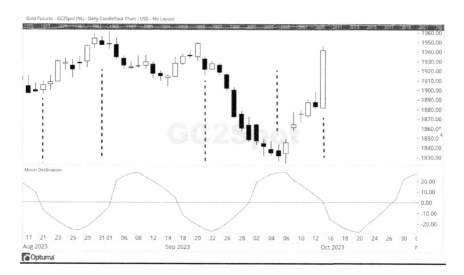

Figure 5-13
Moon Declination and Gold

To assist you with some back-testing of your own, consider that in 2022:

Moon was at its **maximum** declination: January 17, February 13, March 12, April 8, May 6, June 2, July 26, August 23, September 19, October 15, November 13, and December 10.

Moon was at its **minimum** declination: January 30, February 26, March 25, April 22, May 19, June 15, July 13, August 9, September 6, October 3, October 30, November 26, and December 24.

Moon was at **zero** declination: January 8, January 23, February 5, February 20, March 5, March 19, April 1, April 15, April 28, May 12, May 25, June 9, June 21, July 5, July 19, August 3, August 15, August 29, September 11, September 26, October 9, October 23, November 5, November 19, December 2, December 17, and December 30.

In 2023:

Moon was at its **maximum** declination: January 6, February 2, March 2, March 28, April 25, May 22, June 18, July 15, August 12, September 8, October 5, November 2, November 29, and December 26.

Moon was at its **minimum** declination: January 20, February 16, March 15, April 12, May 9, June 5, July 2, July 30, August 27, September 24, October 20, November 16, and December 14.

Moon was at **zero** declination: January 13, January 26, February 9, February 23, March 8, March 22, April 5, April 18, May 2, May 15, May 29, June 11, June 26, July 8, July 23, August 5, August 19, September 1, September 15, September 29, October 13, October 26, November 9, November 23, December 6, and December 20.

For 2024:

Moon will be at **maximum** declination: January 23, February 19, March 18, April 13, May 11, June 7, July 5, August 1, August 28, September 24, October 21, November 18, and December 16.

Moon will be at **minimum** declination: January 10, February 6, March 5, April 1, April 28, May 25, June 22, July 19, August 16, September 12, October 9, November 5, December 3, and December 30.

Moon will be at **zero** declination: January 3, 16 and 30, February 13, March 11, April 7, May 4, June 1 and 28, July 12 and 25, August 8 and 21, September 4 and 18, October 1, 16, and 29, November 11, and December 22.

Individual planets experience declinations of up to about 25 degrees above and below the ecliptic plane. My introduction to planetary declination came several years ago with the discovery of a 25-year-old astrology book in a used bookshop. [4] The book suggested focusing on the planetary declination levels that were in place at the date a stock or commodity futures contract first started trading on an exchange (first trade date). It is possible that this approach was gleaned from the work of W.D. Gann.

In his 1927 book, *Tunnel Through the Air,* [5] Gann references days when the story's hero, Robert Gordon, was very certain trend changes would occur on his Major Motors stock. Gann hints strongly to watch for Mars and Venus to pass the same declination level as they were at on the first trade date (their natal declination levels). When I checked the Mars and Venus planetary declination at the Major Motors first trade date cited in the book and compared those figures to Robert Gordon's key dates, I found a correlation. Mr. Gann's book is more than just an interesting story. It is a resource of valuable information, carefully concealed in plain view.

Venus and Mars Natal Declination Transits

As Gann's 1927 book hints, dates when Venus and Mars pass through their natal declination levels are critical dates to pay attention to when trading commodity futures contracts and stocks. Historical declination data is readily available on the internet. Or, a software program such as Solar Fire Gold will also help you identify the data. Just remember—use heliocentric data when examining declination dates.

Consider the following examples:

Gold

On December 31, 1974 when the Gold futures instrument was launched, Venus was -20 degrees declination and Mars was also -20 degrees.

Venus appears to be the planet to watch when it comes to Gold futures pricing. In 2022, Venus recorded three transits of the -20 degree declination level. All three events aligned to inflection points on the price chart.

In 2023, Venus passed through its December 31, 1974 natal declination levels (+/- 1.5 degrees tolerance) as follows:

- ☿ June 22 to July 1
- ☿ August 3 to August 8.

In late June, 2023 Gold price recorded a significant low at the $1900 per ounce level. This aligns to Venus being at -20 degrees of declination. In early August, Gold prices were already in a bearish decline and Venus passing its natal declination was not powerful enough to disrupt the trend.

For 2024, Venus will be at its December 31, 1974 natal declination level:

- ☿ **February 2 to February 10**
- ☿ **March 16 to March 23**
- ☿ **September 14 to September 23**
- ☿ **October 26 to November 3.**

Crude Oil

WTI Crude Oil futures started trading in New York on March 30, 1983. At that date, Venus was +24 degrees of declination and Mars was +13 degrees of declination.

In 2022, Venus was at its natal declination level (+24 degrees) from January 1 to 12, 2022 and August 3 to 26, 2022. Mars was at its natal declination level (+13 degrees) from September 21 to October 4.

Mars seems to be the planet to watch when it comes to Oil pricing. Oil recorded a swing pivot in late September 2022 which set the stage for a $15 per barrel rally.

For 2023, Mars was at its 1983 first trade declination level from May 5 to 19. Just as Mars was about to revisit its natal declination, Oil price recorded a significant low at the $67.50 level.

For 2024, Mars will be at its March 30, 1983 natal declination levels:

☼ **August 8 to August 18.**

Soybeans

The Chicago Board of Trade was founded April 3, 1848. W.D. Gann was very cognizant of this date when trading Soybeans. Looking at Soybean futures through the lens of this date, as opposed to the 1936 date when Soybean futures actually started trading, yields some interesting finds.

At the 1848 date, Venus was at -22 degrees of declination and Mars was at +22 degrees of declination.

In 2022, Venus passed its natal declination level between April 4th and 15th giving rise to a $1.40 per bushel rally. Venus again passed this declination level from May 7 to May 16. The notable feature in this timeframe was a swing low. Two more transits occurred November 15 to 29 and December 11 to 24.

In 2022, Mars passed its natal declination level (+22 degrees) between November 10 and December 7. The start of this declination transit stirred traders' emotions and Soybeans broke free from a consolidation pattern on the price chart.

In 2023, Venus was at the -22-degree level of natal declination from June 27 to July 10 and July 25 to August 6. These two timeframes collaborated to form a double-top formation on the chart.

Mars was at the +22-degree level of natal declination from February 1 through March 13. This declination transit marked a topping pattern on the chart.

For 2024 Mars and Venus will be at their April 3, 1848 natal declination levels:

- ✿ **March 6 to 19 (Venus)**
- ✿ **September 15 to 29 (Venus)**
- ✿ **October 25 to 28 (Venus)**
- ✿ **September 26 to October 30 (Mars)**

Gann's other date that he used was October 5, 1936 when the Soybean futures contract first started trading in Chicago. At that date, Mars was at +18 degrees of declination and Venus was at -22 degrees of declination.

In 2022, Mars passed through the +18 level of declination level between October 16 to November 1. This triggered Soybeans to break out of a sideways pattern on the chart.

In 2022, Venus passed through -22 degrees of declination between April 2 and 15, May 2 and 15, and November 15 and 28. The April event kick-started a rally. The May event aligned to a swing pivot low. The November transit aligned to a rally.

In 2023, Mars passed its natal declination level from March 27 to April 18. A swing bottom can be seen at the start of this transit.

In 2023, Venus passed through -22 degrees declination between June 27 and July 10, and November 14-27. Soybean price recorded a significant peak on July 3.

For 2024, Mars and Venus will be at their October 1936 natal declination levels:

- ☼ **February 7 to 19 (Venus)**
- ☼ **March 6 to 14 (Venus)**
- ☼ **September 19 to October 2 (Venus)**
- ☼ **October 17 to 28 (Venus)**
- ☼ **September 2 to 14 (Mars).**

NYSE

The New York Stock Exchange (NYSE) can also be viewed through the lens of declination. As the next chapter will reveal, the NYSE traces its origins to May 17, 1792. At that date Venus was at -2 degrees declination and Mars was at -9 degrees of declination.

In 2023, Mars passed its natal declination level from September 5 to 21. The S&P 500 faded by 160 points as a result.

In 2023, Venus passed its natal declination level on three occasions, January 24 to February 1, May 21 to 26, and September 8 -12. The late January transit triggered the start of a sell-off. The end of the May transit sparked a rally that lasted into early August. The September transit marked the start of a bearish decline.

For 2024 Mars and Venus will be at their May 17, 1792 natal declination levels:

- ☼ **January 1 to 5 (Venus)**
- ☼ **April 19 to 25 (Venus)**
- ☼ **August 11 to 17 (Venus)**
- ☼ **November 29 to December 5 (Venus)**
- ☼ **May 12 to 23 (Mars).**

In Chapter Seven, a variety of commodity futures products will be discussed. Natal declination levels will be provided as part of each individual discussion.

CHAPTER SIX

Lunar Cycles and Equity Markets

The Lunation and the New York Stock Exchange (NYSE)

In our hyper-linked economy, events on the New York Stock Exchange can quickly reverberate across other global exchanges. It is for this reason that all of my Almanacs to date have focused on the New York Exchange.

No examination of the astrology of the New York Stock Exchange would be complete without mention once again of Louise McWhirter. After years of reading old papers and manuscripts, I still have no idea who Louise McWhirter was. What I *do* know is that Louise McWhirter focused not only on the 18.6-year cycle, but also on the astrology of the New York Exchange. Her technique, which revolves around the New Moon (lunation), remains viable to this day.

One observation of interest pertains to the actions of the Federal Reserve in the aftermath of the COVID-19 panic selloff. Massive amounts of fiat liquidity were pumped into the banking system to lift the economy and the markets. This liquidity partly obscured any weakness on equity markets with "buy the dip" being the resounding cry when markets expressed weakness. The Federal Reserve reined in its liquidity injections in early 2022 to quell inflation. Almost immediately, astrology in general, and the McWhirter method in particular started to again correlate to market movements.

Lunation is the astrological term for a New Moon. At a lunation, the Sun and Moon are separated by 0-degrees and are together in the same sign of the zodiac. The correlation between the monthly lunation event and New York Stock Exchange price movements was first popularized in 1937 by McWhirter. In her book, *Theory of Stock Market Forecasting,* (1) she discussed how a lunation exhibiting hard aspects to planets such as Mars, Jupiter, Saturn, Neptune, and Uranus was indicative of a lunar cycle during which the New York Stock Exchange would display notable volatility. In particular, she also paid close attention to Mars and Neptune, the two planets that rule the New York Stock Exchange.

The concept of planetary rulership extends back to the 1800s when astrologers began denoting each zodiac sign as having a celestial body that ruled that sign. The planetary placements at the day and time the New York Stock Exchange was founded in 1792 were such that Mars and Neptune were the rulers of the zodiac at that moment. This is because the 10th House of the NYSE birth horoscope spans the signs of Pisces and Aries. Neptune rules Pisces and Mars rules Aries. McWhirter said those times of a lunar month when the transiting Moon makes 0-degree aspects to the 1792 natal locations of Mars and Neptune should be watched carefully.

New York Stock Exchange – First Trade Chart

The New York Stock Exchange officially opened for business on May 17, 1792. As the horoscope in Figure 6-1 shows, the NYSE has its

Ascendant (Asc) at 14-degrees of Cancer and its Mid-Heaven (MC) at 24-degrees of Pisces.

McWhirter further paid close attention to those times in the monthly lunar cycle when the transiting Moon passed by the NYSE natal Asc and MC locations at 14 Cancer and 24 Pisces respectively.

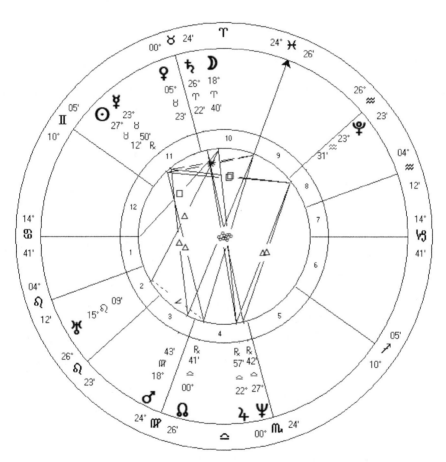

Figure 6-1
NYSE First Trade horoscope

The McWhirter Methodology

In my research and writing, I follow the McWhirter methodology for shorter-term trend changes. When forecasting whether or not a coming month will be volatile or not for the NYSE, the McWhirter methodology starts with creating a horoscope chart for the New Moon date and positioning the Ascendant of the chart at 14-degrees Cancer (the Ascendant position on the 1792 natal chart of the New York Stock Exchange). Positioning the Ascendant is made easy with clicks of the mouse when using the *Solar Fire Gold* software program. Aspects to the lunation are then studied. If the lunation is at a 0, 90, or 120-degree aspect to 14 of Cancer, or 24 of Pisces, one can expect a volatile month ahead. A lack of such aspects portends a less volatile period.

The McWhirter method further demands a consideration of the degree location of the Moon each day. Aspects of the transiting Moon to the natal Mars point at 18 Virgo, the natal Neptune point at 27 Libra, the natal Ascendant point at 14 Cancer, or the natal Mid-Heaven point at 24 Pisces all represent dates of potential short-term trend reversals. Although not expressly stated by McWhirter, it is also important to pay attention to those dates when Moon is at either maximum or minimum declination. As well, dates when Mercury is retrograde and dates when Venus and Mars are at or near their maximum or minimum declination should also be considered carefully.

Similarly, when studying an individual stock or an individual commodity futures contract, the McWhirter approach calls for the creation of a horoscope chart at the first trade date of the stock or commodity. The Ascendant is then shifted so that the Sun is at the Ascendant. The software program *Solar Fire Gold* is very good for generating first trade horoscope charts for McWhirter analysis where the Ascendant needs to be shifted. As to why she placed the Sun at the Ascendant for an individual stock and 14 of Cancer at the Ascendant for analyzing a lunation event, remains unclear to me.

In stock and commodity analyses, McWhirter paid strict attention to those times of a calendar year when transiting Sun, Mars, Jupiter, Saturn, Neptune, and Uranus made hard 0, 90, and 180-degree aspects to the natal Mid-Heaven, natal Ascendant, natal Sun, natal Jupiter, and even the natal Moon of the individual stock or commodity future being studied.

One must be alert at these aspects for the possibility of a trend change, the possibility of increased volatility within a trend, or even the possibility of a breakout from a chart consolidation pattern. Evidence of such trend changes will be found by applying chart technical indicators as discussed in Chapter Two.

February-March 2020: A Historical Example

The McWhirter method can be thoroughly appreciated by examining events around the 2020 COVID panic sell-off which started in late February:

- ✿ A New Moon on February 23, 2020 came during Mercury retrograde

- ✿ Within a day of the New Moon, the Moon transited past the NYSE natal Mid-Heaven (24 Pisces).

- ✿ A day later, Moon made a hard 90-degree aspect to the natal Ascendant at 14 Cancer. Saturn was 90-degrees square the NYSE 1792 natal Saturn point and Jupiter was 120 degrees (trine) to the 1792 natal Mars point.

- ✿ On February 27, Moon transited past the natal Moon. On March 1, Moon transited past the natal Sun location.

- ✿ On March 4, Moon transited past the natal Ascendant point.

☼ On March 9, Moon transited past the natal Mars location. On March 12, Moon transited past the natal Neptune location.

☼ On March 24, the lunar cycle ended and a New Moon event materialized. The S&P 500 reached a low point and began to recover.

As a trader or investor, you can view the events of February-March, 2020 through the lens of the Federal Reserve and fiat stimulus or you can view the events through the lens of the New Moons and aspects to key NYSE natal zodiac points. True, the Federal Reserve did unleash stimulus measures designed to prop up the markets. But the McWhirter method provides day by day insight into market behavior.

What follows is a listing of the date for each lunar cycle in 2024 along with a list of times when Moon passes Mars, Neptune, the NYSE natal Mid-Heaven at 24 Pisces, and the NYSE natal Ascendant at 14 Cancer. In addition, dates of planetary retrograde, dates of declination maxima and minima, and dates of planetary elongation are included.

2024 Lunation Events – S&P 500

January 2024-February 2024

Market action in January 2024 will be influenced by the New Moon cycle that commences on January 11 (Sun at 21 Capricorn) and runs to February 9, 2024 when Sun will be at 20 Aquarius. As this lunation gets underway, Venus will have crossed through its zero-degree declination level—an indicator of a trend change. The lunation is just within orb of being 90-degrees square to the natal Neptune point. In addition, Moon is at its declination minimum at this lunation which also supports the narrative for a trend change. Mid-month, Mercury will be at its greatest westerly elongation—another indicator of a short term trend change. Expect a volatile lunar cycle.

Key dates during this lunar cycle are:

- ✿ January 12: Mercury at greatest westerly elongation
- ✿ January 16: Moon passes natal Mid-Heaven at 24 Pisces
- ✿ January 16: Moon at 0-degrees declination
- ✿ January 18: Moon passes natal Moon.
- ✿ January 20: Moon passes natal Sun position
- ✿ January 22: Mars is at its declination minimum
- ✿ January 24: Moon passes natal Ascendant
- ✿ January 24: Moon at declination maximum
- ✿ January 26: Moon Void of Course (VOC)
- ✿ January 29: Moon passes natal Mars location
- ✿ January 30: Moon at 0-degrees declination
- ✿ January 30-31: Federal Open Market Committee (FOMC) Meeting to set the key lending rate
- ✿ February 1-2: Moon passes natal Neptune while Mercury is at aphelion
- ✿ February 6: Moon at declination minimum.

February-March 2024

Market action through the remainder of February and into March 2024 will be influenced by the New Moon cycle which commences on February 9, 2024 and runs until March 10 (Sun at 20 Pisces). The lunation is within orb of being 90-degrees square to the natal Sun. Venus making its declination minimum during this cycle suggests added volatility.

Key dates during this lunar cycle are:

- ✿ February 12-13: Moon passes natal Mid-Heaven and is at 0-degrees declination

- ✿ February 14: Moon passes natal Moon

- ✿ February 16: Moon passes natal Sun location

- ✿ February 16: Moon VOC

- ✿ February 19-20: Moon at declination maximum and passes natal Ascendant

- ✿ February 25: Moon passes natal Mars location and is at 0-degrees declination

- ✿ February 26: Venus is at its exact declination minimum

- ✿ February 27: Moon VOC

- ✿ February 28: Moon passes natal Neptune location

- ✿ March 4: Moon VOC

- ✿ March 5: Moon at declination minimum

- ✿ March 6: Moon VOC

- ✿ March 8: Moon VOC.

March-April 2024

Market action through March and into April 2024 will be influenced by the New Moon cycle which commences early on March 10, 2024 and runs until April 8 (Sun at 19 Aries). This lunation is situated within a few degrees of the 1792 NYSE natal Mid-Heaven location. As well, Moon is at 0-degrees declination at this lunation. This is all suggestive of added volatility on the equity market. Supporting this observation is the Mercury greatest elongation event in late March and the Mercury retrograde event that starts at month end.

Key dates during this lunar cycle are:

- ✿ March 12: Moon passes natal Moon

- ✿ March 12: Moon VOC

- ✿ March 13: Sun at NYSE natal Mid-Heaven

- ✿ March 14: Moon passes natal Sun location

- ✿ March 17: Mercury at perihelion

- ✿ March 18: Moon at declination maximum and passes by the natal Ascendant point

- ✿ March 19-20: FOMC Meeting

- ✿ March 23-24: Moon passes natal Mars location and is at 0-degrees declination

- ✿ March 24: Mercury at greatest easterly elongation

- ✿ March 26: Moon at natal Neptune location

- ✿ March 29: Moon VOC

- ✿ April 1: Moon at declination minimum

- ✿ April 1: Mercury turns retrograde.

April-May 2024

Market action through April will be influenced by the lunation cycle that runs April 8 to May 7, 2024. The lunation comes just as Moon is at 0-degrees declination. This is suggestive of added volatility. As was noted in an earlier chapter, Professor Weston's work calls for a market maxima point in April 2024. As well, Mercury will be retrograde for a good portion of this lunar cycle. With Mercury retrograde, one should expect the unexpected.

Key dates during this lunar cycle are:

- ☼ April 8: Moon passes natal Moon

- ☼ April 11: Moon passes natal Sun location

- ☼ April 13-14: Moon at declination maximum and at natal Ascendant

- ☼ April 20-21: Moon at natal Mars location and at 0-degrees declination

- ☼ April 18-28: Mars passes the NYSE natal Mid-Heaven

- ☼ April 23: Moon passes natal Neptune location

- ☼ April 24: Mercury retrograde complete

- ☼ April 24: Venus passes through 0-degrees of declination

- ☼ April 28: Moon at declination minimum

- ☼ April 30: Mercury at aphelion

- ☼ April 30-May 1: FOMC Meeting

- ☼ May 2: Moon VOC

- ☼ May 4: Moon passes natal Mid-Heaven point and is at 0-degrees declination

- ☼ May 4 to 26: Jupiter passing NYSE natal Sun location

- ☼ May 6: Moon passes natal Moon.

May-June 2024

Market action through May will be influenced by the lunation cycle that runs May 7 through June 6, 2024. The lunation is 120-degrees trine to the natal Mars location. This suggests added volatility during this lunar cycle. The Mercury greatest elongation event will also add some volatility and possibly a trend change.

Key dates during this lunar cycle are:

- ⚙ May 8: Moon passes natal Sun location

- ⚙ May 9: Mercury at greatest westerly elongation

- ⚙ May 11: Moon at natal Ascendant and at declination maximum

- ⚙ May 15: Moon VOC

- ⚙ May 17: Moon at natal Mars location and at 0-degrees declination.

- ⚙ May 19: Sun at NYSE natal Sun

- ⚙ May 20: Moon passes natal Neptune location

- ⚙ May 25: Moon at declination minimum

- ⚙ May 29: Moon VOC

- ⚙ May 31-June 1: Moon passes natal Mid-Heaven point and is at 0-degrees declination

- ⚙ June 2: Moon passes natal Moon

- ⚙ June 4: Moon passes natal Sun location.

June-July 2024

Market action through June 2024 will be influenced by the New Moon cycle which commences on June 6, 2024 (Sun at 16 Gemini) and runs until July 6 (Sun at 14 Cancer). The lunation is 90-degrees square to the NYSE natal Mars location. This, combined with the Moon being nearly at its declination maximum at the lunation suggests volatility. Venus making its declination maximum mid-way through this cycle supports the volatility narrative.

Key dates during this lunar cycle are:

- ⚙ June 8: Moon at natal Ascendant and at declination maximum

- ☼ June 11-12: FOMC Meeting
- ☼ June 13: Moon at natal Mars location and Mercury at perihelion
- ☼ June 16: Moon at 0-degrees declination and at nata; Neptune location
- ☼ June 18: Venus is at its exact declination maximum
- ☼ June 19: Mars passes through 0-degrees of declination
- ☼ June 22: Moon at declination minimum
- ☼ June 27: Moon at the natal Mid-Heaven
- ☼ June 29: Moon passes natal Moon
- ☼ July 2: Moon at natal Sun location
- ☼ July 2-9: Sun at NYSE natal Asc
- ☼ July 5: Moon at declination maximum and passing the natal Ascendant.

July-August 2024

Market action through July, 2024 will be influenced by the New Moon cycle that commences on July 5, 2024 (Sun at 14 Cancer) and runs at August 4. The lunation being at the NYSE natal Ascendant point is significant and could signal a period of volatile behavior.

Key dates during this lunar cycle are:

- ☼ July 11: Moon at natal Mars location and at 0-degrees declination
- ☼ July 13-25: Mars passes NYSE natal Sun location
- ☼ July 14: Moon passes natal Neptune location
- ☼ July 19: Moon at declination minimum

- ✿ July 22: Mercury at greatest easterly elongation
- ✿ July 23: Moon at natal Pluto location
- ✿ July 25: Moon at natal Mid-Heaven location
- ✿ July 26: Moon passes natal Moon
- ✿ July 27: Mercury at aphelion
- ✿ July 29: Moon at natal Sun location
- ✿ July 30-31: FOMC Meeting
- ✿ August 1-2: Moon at natal Ascendant and at declination maximum.

August-September 2024

Market action through August 2024 will be influenced by the New Moon cycle that commences on August 4 (Sun at 12 Leo) and runs until September 3 (Sun at 11 Virgo). The lunation itself is not at any malefic (harmful) aspects to other planets. However, Mercury retrograde might provide some drama during the lunar cycle.

Key dates during this lunar cycle are:

- ✿ August 5: Mercury turns retrograde
- ✿ August 5: Moon VOC
- ✿ August 7: Moon at natal Mars location and closing in on 0-degrees declination
- ✿ August 10: Moon at the natal Neptune location
- ✿ August 21: Moon at natal Mid-Heaven and also at 0-degrees declination
- ✿ August 23: Moon passes natal Moon
- ✿ August 23: Moon VOC
- ✿ August 25: Moon at natal Sun location

- ✿ August 27: Mercury retrograde finished
- ✿ August 28: Moon at natal Ascendant location and declination maximum.

September-October 2024

Market action through September 2024 will be influenced by the New Moon cycle that commences on September 3 (Sun at 11 Virgo) and runs until October 2 (Sun at 9 Libra). The lunation is within orb of being conjunct the 1792 NYSE natal Mars location. The cycle starts off with Mercury at its greatest westerly elongation. As well, Moon will also be at 0-degrees declination at the lunation. This all implies some volatility during this lunar cycle.

Key dates during this lunar cycle are:

- ✿ September 4: Mercury at greatest westerly elongation
- ✿ September 6-14: Sun passes NYSE natal Mars location
- ✿ September 7: Moon passes natal Neptune location
- ✿ September 9: Mercury Perihelion
- ✿ September 12: Moon at declination minimum
- ✿ September 16: Moon at natal Pluto location
- ✿ September 17-18: FOMC Meeting
- ✿ September 18: Moon at natal Mid-Heaven and at 0-degrees declination
- ✿ September 19: Moon passes natal Moon
- ✿ September 24: Moon at declination maximum
- ✿ September 24-October 5: Mars passes NYSE natal Ascendant

- ☼ September 26: Moon at natal Mid-Heaven
- ☼ September 30: Moon at the natal Mars location
- ☼ October 1: Moon at 0-degrees declination.

October-November 2024

Market action through October will be influenced by the New Moon cycle that commences on October 2 (Sun at 9 Libra) and runs until October 31 (Sun at 9 Scorpio). This lunation is at a hard 90-degree square aspect to the natal Ascendant point. This suggests added market volatility. Moon is also at 0-degrees declination at this lunation which could stir up further volatility. As was noted in an earlier chapter, Professor Weston's work called for a market maxima in November 2024. Oftentimes his maxima points can occur several weeks earlier (or later) than calculated. Given the cosmic energy associated with this October lunation, one should be alert to the possibility of a trend reversal point.

Key dates during this lunar cycle are:

- ☼ October 4: Moon passes natal Neptune location
- ☼ October 8: Venus is at its declination minimum
- ☼ October 9: Moon is at declination minimum
- ☼ October 13: Moon is at natal Pluto location
- ☼ October 15-16: Moon passes natal Mid-Heaven, natal Moon, and is at 0-degrees declination
- ☼ October 17-15: Sun passes NYSE natal Neptune location
- ☼ October 19: Moon at natal Sun location
- ☼ October 21: Moon at declination maximum
- ☼ October 23: Moon at natal Ascendant and Mercury is at aphelion

- ☼ October 28-29: Moon at natal Mars location and 0-degrees declination
- ☼ October 31: Moon at natal Neptune location.

November-December 2024

Market action through November 2024 will be influenced by the New Moon cycle which commences on November 1 (Sun at 9 Scorpio) and runs until November 30 (Sun at 9 Sagittarius). The lunation is *not* at any detrimental aspect to key points in the 1792 NYSE natal horoscope wheel. However, Mars will be making its declination maximum during the entire month. This suggests a trend change could be in store.

Key dates during this lunar cycle are:

- ☼ November 5: Moon at declination minimum
- ☼ November 6: Mercury turns retrograde
- ☼ November 6-7: FOMC Meeting
- ☼ November 11: Moon at natal Mid-Heaven and at 0-degrees declination
- ☼ November 13: Moon passes natal Moon
- ☼ November 15: Moon at natal Sun location
- ☼ November 16: Mercury at greatest easterly elongation
- ☼ November 18-19: Moon at natal Ascendant and at declination maximum
- ☼ November 22: Moon VOC
- ☼ November 24-25: Moon natal Mars location and at 0-degrees declination
- ☼ November 27: Moon at natal Neptune location
- ☼ November 27: Moon VOC.

December 2024

Market action through December 2024 will be influenced by the New Moon cycle that commences on November 30 and runs until December 29 (Sun at 8 Capricorn). The lunation is *not* at any detrimental aspect to key points in the 1792 horoscope wheel. However, Mercury is retrograde until mid-month which could trigger some drama.

Key dates during this lunar cycle are:

✪ December 3: Moon at declination minimum

✪ December 6: Mercury at perihelion

✪ December 8: Moon at natal Mid-Heaven

✪ December 10: Moon passes natal Moon

✪ December 13: Moon at the natal Sun location

✪ December 14: Mercury retrograde finishes

✪ December 16: Moon passes natal Ascendant and is at declination maximum

✪ December 17-18: FOMC Meeting

✪ December 21-22: Moon at natal Mars location and 0-degrees declination

✪ December 24: Moon at natal Neptune location

✪ December 24: Mercury at greatest westerly elongation

✪ December 27: Moon VOC

✪ December 30: Moon at declination minimum

✪ December 30: New Moon at 9 Capricorn and a New Year begins.

2024 Lunation Events – Nasdaq

In this edition of the *Financial Astrology Almanac*, I have decided to add a McWhirter-type analysis for the Nasdaq exchange which traces its origins to February 8, 1971. Figure 6-2 illustrates the planetary placements at that date assuming a 9:17 am first trade. Normally, one would expect the first trade to be at the 9:30 am hour to match the NYSE. However, it is very likely that at this first trade date a trade was allowed to go through at 9:17 am.

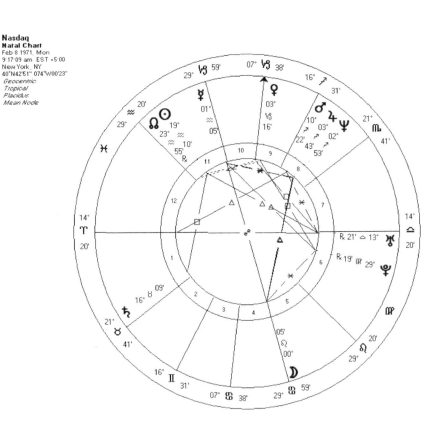

Figure 6-2
Nasdaq first trade horoscope

This would place the Ascendant at a hard 90-degree aspect to the NYSE Ascendant point. The Mid-Heaven is at 7 of Capricorn which makes Saturn the ruling planet for Nasdaq. In addition, on February 8, 1971 Mars was at its minimum declination level.

What follows is a listing of the dates in each lunar cycle of 2024 along with dates when Moon passes the Ascendant, Mid-Heaven, and the natal Moon, natal Jupiter, and natal Mercury points. Note in Figure 6-2 how these three celestial bodies form an isosceles triangle pattern in the horoscope wheel.

January 2024-February 2024

Market action in January 2024 will be influenced by the New Moon cycle that commences on January 11 (Sun at 21 Capricorn) and runs to February 9, 2024 when Sun will be at 20 Aquarius. The lunation is just within orb of being conjunct to the Nasdaq natal Mid-Heaven at 10-degrees of Capricorn. This is suggestive of an energized lunar cycle. As this lunation gets underway, Venus will have just crossed through its zero-degree declination level – a strong indicator of a trend change. In addition, Moon is at its declination minimum at this lunation which also supports the narrative for a trend change

Key dates during this lunar cycle are:

- ✿ January 12-13: Moon passes natal Mercury and natal Sun locations
- ✿ January 13-22: Mars at Nasdaq natal Mid-Heaven
- ✿ January 17: Moon passes the natal Ascendant location and is at 0-degrees declination
- ✿ January 23: Moon at declination maximum
- ✿ January 25: Moon at natal Moon, Mars at its declination minimum

- ☼ January 26: Moon VOC
- ☼ January 26: Mars reaches it declination minimum level
- ☼ January 30: Moon at 0-degrees declination
- ☼ January 30-31: FOMC meets
- ☼ February 4: Moon at natal Jupiter
- ☼ February 4-12: Sun passing Nasdaq natal Sun location
- ☼ February 6: Moon at declination minimum
- ☼ February 7: Moon passes natal Mid-Heaven
- ☼ February 8: Moon at natal Mercury location.

February 2024-March 2024

Market action through the remainder of February and into March 2024 will be influenced by the New Moon cycle which commences on February 9, 2024 and runs until March 10 (Sun at 20 Pisces). The lunation is conjunct to the Nasdaq natal Sun which suggests a lunar cycle of heightened volatility. Venus making its declination minimum late during this cycle suggests added volatility.

Key dates during this lunar cycle are:

- ☼ February 13: Moon passes natal Ascendant and is at 0-degrees declination
- ☼ February 19: Moon at declination maximum
- ☼ February 21: Moon passes natal Moon location
- ☼ February 25: Venus at its declination minimum
- ☼ February 26: Moon at 0-degrees declination
- ☼ February 27: Moon VOC
- ☼ March 2: Moon at the natal Jupiter location

- ✿ March 3-14: Mars passing the Nasdaq natal Sun location
- ✿ March 4: Moon VOC
- ✿ March 5: Moon at natal Mid-Heaven
- ✿ March 6: Moon passes natal Mercury location and is at minimum declination
- ✿ March 6: Moon VOC
- ✿ March 8: Moon passes natal Sun.
- ✿ March 8: Moon VOC.

March – April 2024

Market action through March and into April 2024 will be influenced by the New Moon cycle which commences early on March 10, 2024 and runs until April 8 (Sun at 19 Aries). This lunation is not in any detrimental aspect to key features of the Nasdaq natal chart. However, Mars is conjunct the natal Sun which suggests added energy will be on full display. Supporting this observation is the Mercury greatest elongation event in late March and the Mercury retrograde event that starts at month end.

Key dates during this lunar cycle are:

- ✿ March 12: Moon passes natal Ascendant
- ✿ March 12: Moon VOC
- ✿ March 19: Moon at declination maximum and is passing natal Moon
- ✿ March 19-20: FOMC meets
- ✿ March 29: Moon passes natal Jupiter location and is at 0-degrees declination
- ✿ March 29: Moon VOC

✿ April 1: Moon at declination minimum and passing the natal Mid-Heaven

✿ April 3: Moon at natal Mercury location

✿ April 4: Moon passes natal Sun

✿ April 4-12: Sun passes Nasdaq natal Ascendant location.

April-May 2024

Market action through April will be influenced by the lunation cycle that runs April 8 to May 7, 2024. The lunation comes just as Moon is at 0-degrees declination. This is suggestive of added volatility. Mercury will be retrograde for a good portion of this lunar cycle. With Mercury, one should expect the unexpected. This lunation will also feature both Mars and Venus passing through their natal declination points. This is further suggestive of added volatility.

Key dates during this lunar cycle are:

✿ April 13: Moon at declination maximum

✿ April 16: Moon passes natal Moon location

✿ April 19-20: Venus at its natal declination

✿ April 24: Venus at 0-degrees declination

✿ April 26: Moon at natal Jupiter location

✿ April 28: Moon at declination minimum and at natal Mid-Heaven location

✿ April 30: Moon at natal Mercury location

✿ April 30-May 1: FOMC meets

✿ May 2: Moon passes natal Sun

✿ May 2: Moon VOC

- ☼ May 2-5: Mars at its natal declination
- ☼ May 4: Moon at 0-degrees declination
- ☼ May 6: Moon passes natal Ascendant.

May-June 2024

Market action through May will be influenced by the lunation cycle that runs May 7 through June 6, 2024. The lunation is not at aspect with any key features of the Nasdaq natal chart. However, the Mercury greatest elongation event will also add some volatility and possibly a trend change.

Key dates during this lunar cycle are:

- ☼ May 9: Mercury at greatest westerly elongation
- ☼ May 13: Moon passes natal Moon location
- ☼ May 11: Moon at declination maximum
- ☼ May 15: Moon VOC
- ☼ May 17: Moon at 0-degrees declination
- ☼ May 20-29: Mars passes Nasdaq natal Ascendant
- ☼ May 23: Moon passes natal Jupiter location
- ☼ May 25-26: Moon at declination minimum and at natal Mid-Heaven
- ☼ May 27: Moon at natal Mercury location
- ☼ May 28: Moon passes natal Sun location
- ☼ May 29: Moon VOC
- ☼ May 31-June 1: Moon at 0-degrees declination
- ☼ June 2: Moon passes natal Ascendant location.

June-July 2024

Market action through June 2024 will be influenced by the New Moon cycle commencing on June 6, 2024 (Sun at 16 Gemini) and running until July 5 (Sun at 14 Cancer). The lunation is 120-degrees trine to the natal Sun location. This, combined with the Moon being nearly at its declination maximum at the lunation suggests volatility. Venus making its declination maximum and Mars being at 0-degrees declination mid-way through this cycle supports the volatility narrative.

Key dates during this lunar cycle are:

- ✿ June 10: Moon at natal Moon
- ✿ June 11-12: FOMC meets
- ✿ June 12: Moon at natal Moon location
- ✿ June 15: Moon at 0-degrees declination
- ✿ June 18-19: Venus at declination maximum, Mars at 0-degrees declination
- ✿ June 20: Moon at natal Jupiter
- ✿ June 22: Moon at declination minimum and at natal Mid-Heaven
- ✿ June 24: Moon at natal Mercury
- ✿ June 25: Moon at natal Sun
- ✿ June 28: Moon at 0-degrees declination
- ✿ June 29: Moon at the natal Ascendant point.

July-August 2024

Market action through July 2024 will be influenced by the New Moon cycle that commences on July 5, 2024 (Sun at 14 Cancer) and runs at August 4. The lunation is at a hard 90-degree aspect to the natal Ascendant point which implies a measure of added volatility.

Key dates during this lunar cycle are:

- ✿ July 7: Moon at natal Moon
- ✿ July 11: Moon at 0-degrees declination
- ✿ July 17: Moon passes natal Jupiter location
- ✿ July 19: Moon at declination minimum and at the natal Mid-Heaven
- ✿ July 19-26: Sun passes Nasdaq natal Moon location
- ✿ July 21: Moon at natal Mercury
- ✿ July 22: Moon at natal Sun
- ✿ July 25: Moon at 0-degrees declination
- ✿ July 26: Moon at natal Ascendant location
- ✿ July 30-31: FOMC meets
- ✿ August 3: Moon at declination maximum and natal Moon location.

August-September 2024

Market action through August 2024 will be influenced by the New Moon cycle that commences on August 4 (Sun at 12 Leo) and runs until September 3 (Sun at 11 Virgo). The lunation itself is not at any malefic aspects to other planets.

Key dates during this lunar cycle are:

- ✿ August 5: Moon VOC, Mercury retrograde
- ✿ August 7: Moon closing in on 0-degrees declination

- ✿ August 13: Moon at the natal Jupiter location, Venus at 0-degrees declination

- ✿ August 15-16: Venus is at its natal declination level

- ✿ August 16: Moon at natal Mid-Heaven location

- ✿ August 18: Moon at natal Mercury location

- ✿ August 19: Moon at natal Sun location

- ✿ August 21: Moon at 0-degrees declination

- ✿ August 23: Moon at natal Ascendant location

- ✿ August 23: Moon VOC

- ✿ August 29-30: Moon at natal Moon location and declination minimum.

September-October 2024

Market action through September 2024 will be influenced by the New Moon cycle that commences on September 3 (Sun at 11 Virgo) and runs until October 2 (Sun at 9 Libra). The lunation is not at any detrimental aspects to other planets.

Key dates during this lunar cycle are:

- ✿ September 9: Moon passes natal Jupiter location

- ✿ September 12: Moon at declination minimum

- ✿ September 13-14: Moon passes natal Mid-Heaven and natal Mercury

- ✿ September 15: Moon passes natal Sun

- ✿ September 16: Moon at natal Pluto location

- ✿ September 17-18: FOMC meets

- ✪ September 18-19: Moon at 0-degrees declination and natal Ascendant

- ✪ September 24: Moon at declination maximum

- ✪ September 27: Moon at natal Moon location

- ✪ October 1: Moon at 0-degrees declination.

October-November 2024

Market action through October will be influenced by the New Moon cycle that commences on October 2 (Sun at 9 Libra) and runs until October 31 (Sun at 9 Scorpio). This lunation is at a hard 90-degree square aspect to the natal Mid-Heaven point. Moon is also at 0-degrees declination at this lunation.

Key dates during this lunar cycle are:

- ✪ October 7: Moon passes natal Jupiter location, Venus at declination minimum

- ✪ October 9-10: Moon is at declination minimum and natal Mid-Heaven

- ✪ October 11-12: Moon passes natal Mercury and natal Sun locations

- ✪ October 16: Moon at 0-degrees declination

- ✪ October 17: Moon at natal Ascendant location

- ✪ October 21: Moon at declination maximum

- ✪ October 23: Moon at natal Moon location

- ✪ October 25-November 19: Mars passes Nasdaq natal Moon location

- ✪ October 29: Moon at 0-degrees declination.

November-December 2024

Market action through November 2024 will be influenced by the New Moon cycle that commences on November 1 (Sun at 9 Scorpio) and runs until November 30 (Sun at 9 Sagittarius). The lunation is at hard square aspect to Mars.

Key dates during this lunar cycle are:

- ☿ November 3: Moon at natal Jupiter location
- ☿ November 5-6: Moon at declination minimum and at natal Mid-Heaven
- ☿ November 6-7: FOMC meets
- ☿ November 8-9: Moon passes the natal Mercury and natal Sun points
- ☿ November 11: Moon at 0-degrees declination
- ☿ November 13: Moon at natal Ascendant location
- ☿ November 18: Moon at declination maximum
- ☿ November 20: Moon at natal Moon location
- ☿ November 22: Moon VOC
- ☿ November 24-26: Moon at 0-degrees declination, Mars at maximum declination
- ☿ November 27: Moon VOC
- ☿ November 28-December 5: Sun passes Nasdaq natal Mars.

December 2024

Market action through December 2024 will be influenced by the New Moon cycle that commences on November 30 and runs until December

29 (Sun at 8 Capricorn). The lunation is within orb of being conjunct to the natal Jupiter location.

Key dates during this lunar cycle are:

- ☼ December 1: Moon at natal Jupiter location
- ☼ December 2: Moon VOC
- ☼ December 1-2: Venus at its natal declination level
- ☼ December 3: Moon at declination minimum and natal Mid-Heaven
- ☼ December 4: Venus at 0-degrees declination
- ☼ December 5-6: Moon passes natal Mercury and natal Sun locations
- ☼ December 8: Moon at natal Mid-Heaven
- ☼ December 11: Moon at the natal Ascendant location
- ☼ December 13: Moon VOC
- ☼ December 16: Moon passes declination maximum
- ☼ December 17-18: FOMC meets
- ☼ December 18: Moon at natal Moon location
- ☼ December 22: Moon at 0-degrees declination
- ☼ December 27: Moon VOC
- ☼ December 27-January 5, 2025: Sun passes Nasdaq natal Mid-Heaven
- ☼ December 28: Moon at natal Jupiter location
- ☼ December 30: Moon at declination minimum
- ☼ December 30: New Moon at 9 Capricorn and a new year begins.

CHAPTER SEVEN
Cosmic Events and Commodities

Metals

Gold

Investors who own gold coins or perhaps stocks in gold mining companies are accustomed to routinely checking the price of the shiny metal by tuning into a television business channel or perhaps obtaining a live online quote of the Gold futures price. What many do not realize is that quietly working behind the scenes to define the price of the metal is an archaic methodology called the *London Gold Fix*.

The 1919 Gold Fix Date

The London Gold Fix occurs at 10:30 a.m. and 3:00 p.m. local time each business day in London. Participants in the daily fixes are: Barclay's, HSBC, Scotia Mocatta (a division of Scotia Bank of Canada), and Societe Generale. These twice-daily collaborations (some would say collusions) provide a benchmark price that is then used around the globe to settle and mark-to-market the value of all the various Gold-related derivative contracts in existence.

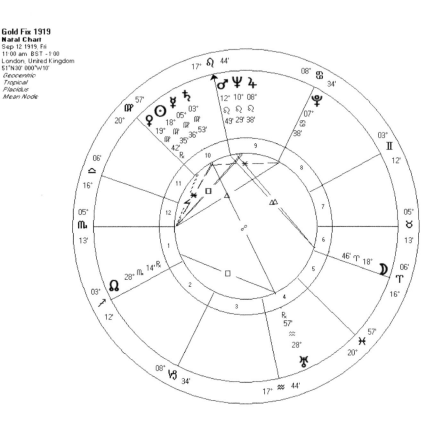

Figure 7-1
1919 London Gold Fix Horoscope

The history of the Gold Fix dates back over one hundred years. On September 12th, 1919, the Bank of England made arrangements with N.M. Rothschild & Sons for the formation of a Gold market in which there would be one official price for Gold bullion quoted on any one day. At 11:00 a.m., the first Gold fixing took place, with the five principal Gold bullion traders and refiners of the day present. These traders and refiners were N.M. Rothschild & Sons, Mocatta & Goldsmid, Pixley & Abell, Samuel Montagu & Co., and Sharps Wilkins.

The horoscope in Figure 7-1 depicts planetary positions at the 1919 Gold Fix creation date. The Ascendant (5 Scorpio), Sun (18 Virgo), and Mid-Heaven (12 Leo) are points to focus on. In particular, attention should be paid to Moon passing these points each month, and on a longer timeframe to Mars passing these points.

Gold investors who have been around for a while will remember the significant $800 per ounce price peak recorded in January 1980. To illustrate how planetary movement is linked to Gold prices, consider that at this price peak, Mars was conjunct the 1919 natal Sun and Moon transited the 1919 natal Moon location less than 2 days after the peak.

As another price peak example, recall that the price of Gold hit a significant peak in early September 2011 at just over $1900 per ounce. At that peak, Mercury had just finished being retrograde and was positioned right at the natal Mid-Heaven point of the 1919 horoscope. Venus was exactly conjunct the 1919 natal Venus point.

In the few weeks that followed this 2011 peak, Gold prices plunged nearly $400 per ounce. But then the Gold price found its legs again and began to rally. This rally is related to Moon passing the 1919 natal Sun point.

In early August 2020, Gold again made a significant high, getting just above $2000 per ounce. Sun conjunct to the 1919 Mid-Heaven played a key role in this price peak. Mars conjunct to the 1919 natal Moon also played a role.

1974 Gold Futures Date

Gold futures contracts started trading in North America on the New York Mercantile Exchange on December 31, 1974. Figure 7-2 illustrates the planetary positions in 1974 at the first trade date of Gold futures.

Embedded in the horoscope is a double-peaked, saw-tooth geometric formation. The apex points are Saturn, Moon, Jupiter, Neptune. The Ascendant is at 4 Aquarius and the Mid-Heaven is at 27 Scorpio. In addition, Sun is at 9 Capricorn.

Note that in the 1919 chart in Figure 7-1, Mars and Neptune are conjunct one another. In the 1974 chart in Figure 7-2, Mars and Neptune are also conjunct one another.

Next, consider why the New York Mercantile Exchange would launch a new futures contract on December 31, a time when most staff would be off for Christmas holidays. If you find this more than a bit odd, you are not alone in your thinking.

Note the location of Moon in the 1974 horoscope at 12 degrees of Leo. Now, look at the 1919 horoscope in Figure 7-1 and observe that 12 degrees of Leo is where Mars and Neptune are located. The 1919 Gold Fix Ascendant is located 90-degrees square to the 1974 futures Ascendant if one assumes a first trade start time of 9:00 a.m. which is a more than reasonable assumption. I take these curious placements as further evidence of a deliberately timed astrological connection between gold price, the 1919 Gold Fix date, and the 1974 first trade date for Gold futures.

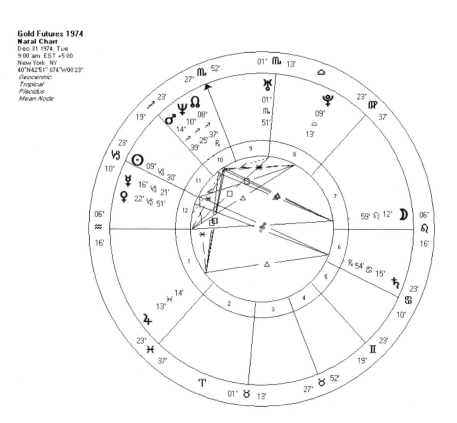

Figure 7-2
Gold futures 1974 First Trade Horoscope

Consider again the significant $800 per ounce price peak reached in January 1980. Sun was conjunct the 1974 natal Sun and Moon was passing the natal Jupiter point.

Consider again the significant peak in early September 2011 at just over $1900 per ounce. Moon passing the 1974 natal Ascendant and Moon passing the natal Saturn point bracket this peak reversal point.

Consider the early August 2020 price peak. Moon was passing the natal Jupiter point and Sun was passing the natal Moon point.

In March 2022, Gold price peaked at just over $2000 per ounce. Moon was at the natal Moon at this point in time.

More recently, in late November 2023, Gold price started to rally as Moon passed the 1974 natal Mid-Heaven point. The rally gathered momentum as both Sun and Mars then transited past the Mid-Heaven point. As I complete the final edits on this manuscript in early December 2023, I note that it is very possible for the positive trend to continue into mid-December when Sun and Mars will complete their transits past natal Neptune, which defines one of the corners of the double-peaked, saw-tooth geometric formation evident in the 1974 natal horoscope wheel.

Such is the intriguing nature of Gold prices. To those readers who are of the opinion that Gold price is manipulated, your notion is indeed a valid one. I believe that planetary cycles are at the core of the secret language being spoken amongst those that play a hand in the price manipulation.

Taking key planetary positions from both the 1919 Gold Fix and 1974 futures horoscopes, the following degree-points are deserving of attention in 2024:

Moon Transits

Using your Ephemeris table, specifically watch for short term trend changes at those times when Moon transits past the following degree intervals:

- ☼ 0 to 10 of Scorpio (1919 Ascendant)

- ☼ 22 Scorpio to 2 Sagittarius (1974 Mid-Heaven)

- ☼ 4 to 14 of Capricorn (1974 natal Sun)

- ☼ 0 to 8 of Aquarius (1974 Ascendant)

- ☼ 13 to 23 of Aries (1919 natal Moon)

- ☼ 3 to 9 of Taurus (square to the 1974 Ascendant)

- ☼ 15 Cancer to 14 Leo (1974 natal Saturn and natal Moon)

- ☼ 13 to 23 of Virgo (1919 natal Sun).

Sun and Mars transits

For 2024:

- ☼ **Mars will transit past the 1974 natal Sun location from January 12-24**

- ☼ **Sun will pass the 1974 natal Ascendant from January 23-30**

- ☼ **Mars will pass the 1974 natal Ascendant point from February 16-27**

- ☼ **Sun will pass the 1974 natal Moon from August 1-8**

- ☼ **Sun will pass the 1974 natal Mid-Heaven November 15-23**

- ☼ **Sun will pass the 1919 natal Moon location from April 4-10**

- ☼ **Mars will pass the 1919 natal Moon location from May 19-30**

- ☼ **Sun will pass the 1919 natal Mid-Heaven from August 5-13**

- ☼ **Sun will pass the 1919 natal Ascendant point from October 24-November 1.**

Declination

On September 12, 1919, when the Gold Fix mechanism was started, Mars was at 23 degrees declination, Venus was at -7 degrees, and Moon was at 0-degrees declination.

For 2024:

- ☿ **Venus will be at -7 degrees declination for several days either side of: January 12, April 12, August 23, and November 25. Mars will be at 23 degrees declination for several days either side October 20**

- ☿ **Moon will be at 0-degrees declination: January 3, 16, and 30, February 13, March 11, April 7, May 4, June 1, and 28, July 12 and 25, August 8 and 21, September 4 and 18, October 1, 16, and 29, November 11, and December 22.**

On December 31, 1974 when Gold futures started trading, Mars was at -20 degrees declination and Venus was at -21 degrees declination. In my opinion, these two planets both being at the same declination level further explains the choice of the unusual date of December 31 as the first trade date.

- ☿ **In 2024, Venus will be at -21 degrees declination for several days either side of: February 7, March 16, September 18, and October 27. Mars will be at -20 degrees declination for several days around March 25.**

Mercury Retrograde

Another valuable tool for Gold traders to consider is Mercury retrograde events. Watch for technical chart trend indicators to suggest a short-term trend change at a retrograde event.

For 2024, Mercury will be:

- ☼ **retrograde from April 1 through April 24**
- ☼ **retrograde from August 5 through August 27**
- ☼ **retrograde from November 26 through December 14.**

Silver

Silver futures started trading on a recognized financial exchange on July 5, 1933. Figure 7-3 shows the First Trade horoscope for silver futures in geocentric format. A first trade time of 9:00 a.m. is assumed.

I am intrigued with this first trade date. Exchange authorities could have started the Silver futures contract trading anytime in 1933. But they focused on July 5, 1933.

July 4, 1776 is a critical date in US history and on this date Sun was at 14 of Cancer. Recall that 14 of Cancer also figures prominently in the first trade horoscope of the NYSE. In 1933, markets would have been closed for the 4th of July celebrations. A first trade date of July 5, is as close as authorities could come to the July 4 date. On July 5, 1933 Sun at 13 degrees is within one degree of the critical 14 of Cancer point. Moreover, Moon (15 Sagittarius), Saturn (15 Aquarius), Mid-Heaven (16 Taurus), and Jupiter (17 Virgo) trace out a 4-sided parallelogram shape. In addition, the Ascendant is at 23 Leo.

Moon Transits

Using your Ephemeris table or software program, specifically watch for those times in each monthly lunar cycle when Moon transits past:

- ☼ 15 Aquarius (natal Saturn)
- ☼ 16 Taurus (natal Mid-Heaven)
- ☼ 23 Leo (natal Ascendant)
- ☼ 17 Virgo (natal Jupiter)
- ☼ 15 Sagittarius (natal Moon).

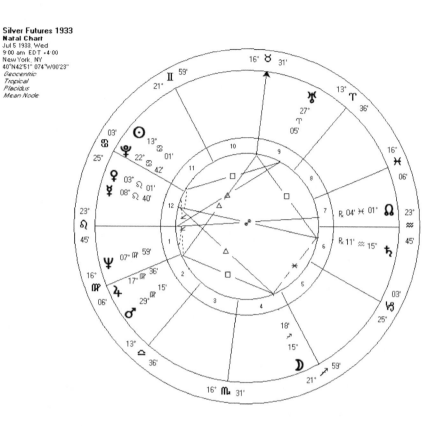

Figure 7-3
Silver futures First Trade Horoscope

My research has further shown that the times when Sun and Mars transit past these various points deserve careful scrutiny for evidence of short term trend changes.

Sun and Mars transits

For 2024:

- ☼ **Mars will pass 15 Aquarius on March 4, and 16 Taurus on July 1.**

- ☼ **Sun will pass 15 Aquarius on February 4, 16 Taurus on May 6, 23 Leo on August 15, 17 Virgo on September 9, and 15 Sagittarius on December 7.**

Declination

Planetary declinations should also be considered when studying price action of Silver futures. In particular, the declination of Venus, Sun, Moon, and Mars deserve watching. Mars was at -14 degrees declination in 1933 as Silver futures were starting to trade for the very first time. Venus was at +14 degrees declination. Moon was at a declination minimum at this first trade date. Mars and Venus are at what is called *contra-parallel declination* (same degree values, but one planet is positive and above the ecliptic while the other is negative and beneath the ecliptic). This further suggests that the selection of this first trade date was not a random occurrence.

- ☼ **For 2024, Venus will be at +14-degrees declination either side of May 7, July 20, and December 29.**

- ☼ **For 2023, Mars will be at -14-degrees declination for several days either side of April 23.**

- ☼ **For 2024, Moon will be at its minimum declination: January 10, February 6, March 5, April 1, April 28, May 25, June 22, July 19, August 16, September 12, October 9, November 5, December 3, December 30.**

Copper

The first trade date for Copper futures was July 29, 1988. Figure 7-4 illustrates the first trade horoscope. A first trade time of 9:00 a.m. is assumed.

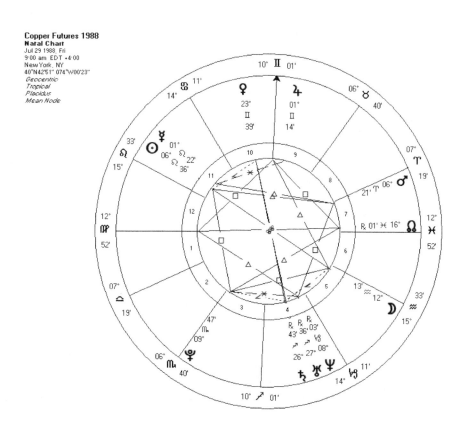

Figure 7-4
Copper futures First Trade Horoscope

The planetary intrigue continues with Copper futures. Notice how Pluto, Neptune, Mars, and Sun trace out a perfect 4-sided parallelogram shape.

In addition to the parallelogram shape, two other points of interest are the Ascendant at 12 Virgo and the Mid-Heaven at 10 Gemini.

Moon Transits

Using your Ephemeris table or software program, specifically watch for those times in each monthly lunar cycle when Moon transits past:

- ☼ 8 Capricorn (natal Neptune)
- ☼ 6 Aries (natal Mars)
- ☼ 10 Gemini (natal Mid-Heaven)
- ☼ 6 Leo (natal Sun)
- ☼ 12 Virgo (natal Ascendant)
- ☼ 9 Scorpio (natal Pluto).

The times when Sun, and Mars pass the parallelogram corner points, the Mid-Heaven, and the Ascendant also deserve careful scrutiny.

Sun and Mars transits

For 2024:

- ☼ **Sun will be passing 8 Capricorn on January 1 as the New Year starts. Sun will pass 6 Aries on March 26, 10 Gemini on May 31, 6 Leo on July 28, 12 Virgo on September 4, and 9 Scorpio on November 9.**

- ☼ **Mars will pass 8 Capricorn on January 15, 6 Aries on April 12, 10 Gemini on August 4, and 6 Leo on December 3. Mars will then turn retrograde.**

Inferior Conjunction

This horoscope wheel features an inferior conjunction of Mercury in the sign of Leo. Also, notice in this horoscope that the first trade date is that of a Full Moon (Sun and Moon are opposite each other in the horoscope).

An inferior conjunction of Mercury marks the start of a new Mercury cycle around the Sun. Mercury inferior conjunction events always occur in association with Mercury being retrograde.

Mercury Retrograde

Back testing has shown a strong correlation between Mercury retrograde events and swing pivot points on Copper futures price charts. This was again observed in 2023 when Copper futures recorded a reversal swing high in early January at retrograde. A handful of days after the retrograde event in May, Copper prices recorded a swing low on the price chart. Prior to the August-September retrograde event, it appeared as though Copper prices were about to rally. The retrograde event put an end to that idea.

For 2024, Mercury will be:

- ✿ **retrograde from April 1 through April 24**
- ✿ **retrograde from August 5 through August 27**
- ✿ **retrograde from November 26 through December 14.**

Declination

At the 1988 first trade date, Mars was at -14 degrees of declination. Venus was at -13 degrees of declination. A first trade date where the declinations of these two planets are within a degree of each other is more than just a little intriguing.

To illustrate the connection between Copper prices and transits of natal declination points, consider that in 2022, Mars was at -14 degrees of declination around June 10. This marked the start of a $1.30 per pound price slide which devastated shares in Copper-mining companies. In 2022, the various times when Venus was at -13 degrees declination all corresponded to pivot points on the price chart.

Mars was again at -14 degrees declination in mid-October 2023. This sparked a $0.40 per pound rally on Copper futures prices.

In 2024:

- ✪ **Mars will be at its 1988 natal declination level for several days on either side of April 25.**

- ✪ **Venus will be at its 1988 natal declination level around: January 19, April 5, September 1, and November 16.**

Platinum

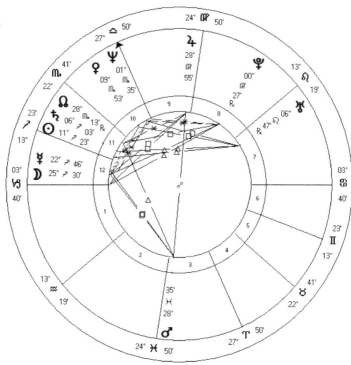

Figure 7-5
Platinum First Trade Horoscope

Platinum futures started trading in New York on December 3, 1956. Assuming an 8:50 a.m. first trade transaction, note the alignment of the IC point to 24 Pisces, which happens to also be the NYSE natal Mid-Heaven point.

In the natal horoscope, Mars (28 Pisces), Jupiter (28 Virgo), and Node (28 Scorpio) form a right-angled triangle pattern. In addition, the Mid-Heaven is at 27 Libra and the Ascendant is at 3 Capricorn.

My research has shown that the times when Moon, Sun, and Mars transit past these triangle corner points, past the Mid-Heaven, and past the Ascendant deserve careful scrutiny.

Moon Transits

Using your Ephemeris table or software program, specifically watch for those times in each monthly lunar cycle when Moon transits past:

- ☼ 28 Pisces (natal Mars)
- ☼ 28 Virgo (natal Jupiter)
- ☼ 27 Libra (natal Mid-Heaven)
- ☼ 28 Scorpio (natal Node)
- ☼ 3 Capricorn (natal Ascendant).
- ☼ Sun and Mars transits

For 2024:

- ☼ **Sun will be passing 28 Pisces on March 18, 28 Virgo on September 18, 27 Libra on October 20, 28 Scorpio on November 20, and 3 Capricorn on December 24.**
- ☼ **Mars will pass 3 Capricorn on January 8, and 28 Pisces on April 28.**

Declination

At the 1956 first trade date, Mars was at 14 degrees declination. Venus was at 4 degrees declination.

In 2023, Mars was at its natal declination level in mid-May. This timeframe marked the onset of a decline in price that would shave over $200 per ounce off Platinum prices.

For 2024:

☼ **Mars will be at 14 degrees declination for several days either side of August 19.**

☼ **Venus will be at 4 degrees declination for several days either side of: April 30, August 6, and December 10.**

Palladium

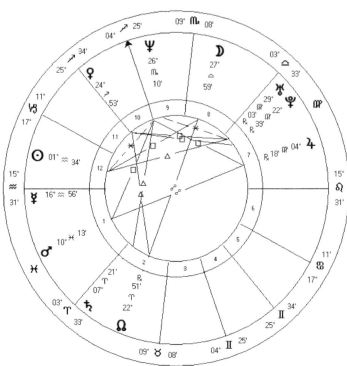

Figure 7-6
Palladium First Trade Horoscope

Palladium futures started trading in New York on January 22, 1968.

Assuming an 8:00 a.m. first trade time, in the natal horoscope Mars (10 Pisces), Jupiter (4 Virgo), and Mid-Heaven (4 Sagittarius) form a right-angled triangle pattern. In addition, the Ascendant is at 15 Aquarius.

My research has shown that the times when Moon, Sun, and Mars transit past these triangle corner points, as well as the Ascendant point, all deserve careful scrutiny.

Moon Transits

Using your Ephemeris table or software program, specifically watch for those times in each monthly lunar cycle when Moon transits past:

- ☿ natal Mars (10 Pisces)
- ☿ natal Jupiter (4 Virgo)
- ☿ natal Mid-Heaven (4 Sagittarius)
- ☿ 15 Aquarius (natal Ascendant).
- ☿ Sun and Mars transits

For 2024:

- ☿ **Sun will be exact at 15 Aquarius on February 4, exact at 10 Pisces on March 1, exact a 4 Virgo on August 26, and exact at 4 Sagittarius on November 25.**
- ☿ **Mars will be exact at 15 Aquarius on March 2. Mars will be exact at 10 Pisces on April 5.**

Declination

On January 22, 1968, Venus was at -9 degrees declination and Mars was at +1 degrees of declination. Moon had just passed the 0-degree declination point.

An examination of these declination levels in 2022 and up to September 2023 show a striking correlation to swing pivot points on the price chart.

For 2024:

- ☼ **Venus will transit past its 1968 natal declination level on January 17, April 8, August 26, and November 20.**

- ☼ **Mars will transit past its 1968 natal declination level on June 25.**

Currencies

Canadian Dollar and British Pound

These two currency futures started trading on May 16th, 1972 on the Chicago Mercantile Exchange. The horoscope in Figure 7-7 illustrates planetary placements at this date. It is interesting to note that Mars is 180-degrees opposite Jupiter. This suggests that Mars and Jupiter may play a role in price fluctuations on these currencies. Mars is also 0-degrees conjunct to Venus, suggesting another cyclical relationship.

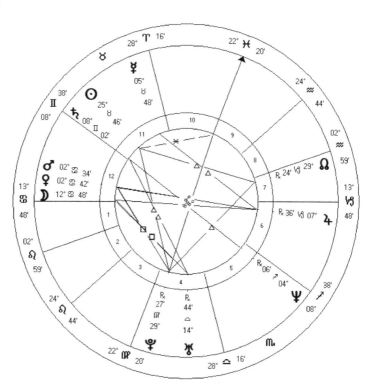

Figure 7-7
British Pound, and Canadian Dollar First Trade Horoscope

Assuming an 8:45 a.m. first trade start time, in the natal horoscope Pluto (29 Virgo), Node (29 Capricorn), and Sun (25 Taurus) form an equilateral triangle pattern. In addition, the Mid-Heaven is at 22 Pisces and the Ascendant is almost at 14 Cancer. I find it fascinating that the Ascendant and Mid-Heaven points closely match those of the NYSE natal horoscope wheel from May 1792.

Moon Transits

Using your Ephemeris table or software program, specifically watch for those times in each monthly lunar cycle when Moon transits past:

- ☼ 25 Taurus (natal Sun)
- ☼ 29 Virgo (natal Pluto)
- ☼ 29 Capricorn (natal Node)
- ☼ 26 Pisces (natal Mid-Heaven)
- ☼ 16 Cancer (natal Ascendant).

My research has further shown that the times when Sun and Mars each transit past these triangle corner points, the Mid-Heaven point, and the Ascendant point, all deserve careful scrutiny.

Sun and Mars transits

For 2024:

- ☼ **Sun will pass 29 Capricorn on January 19, 26 Pisces on March 16, 25 Taurus on May 15, 16 Cancer on July 7, and 29 Virgo on September 21.**

- ☼ **Mars will pass 29 Capricorn on February 12, 26 Pisces on April 25, 25 of Taurus on July 13, and 16 Cancer on October 3.**

Mercury Retrograde

Currency traders should pay close attention to Mercury retrograde events as they show a good alignment to trend changes on the British pound, and Canadian dollar.

For 2024, Mercury will be:

☼ **retrograde from April 1 through April 24**

☼ **retrograde from August 5 through August 27**

☼ **retrograde from November 26 through December 14.**

Declination

At the 1972 first trade date, Mars was at +22 degrees declination, and Venus was at -11 degrees declination. Moon was at its declination maxima.

My back testing has shown a strong correlation with these declination repeats and swing highs and lows on price chart of the Canadian dollar and the British pound.

For 2024:

☼ **Venus will be at its natal declination for several days either side of: January 19, April 7, August 29, and November 16.**

☼ **For 2024, Mars will be at its natal declination for several days either side of August 30, 2024.**

☼ **Moon will be at its declination maximum January 23, February 19, March 18, April 13, May 11, June 7, July 5, August 1, August 28, September 24, October 21, November 18, and December 16.**

Euro Currency

The Euro became the official currency for the European Union on January 1, 2002 when Euro bank notes became freely and widely circulated.

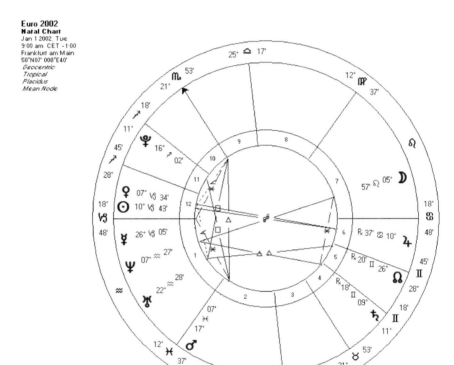

Figure 7-8
Euro Currency First Trade Horoscope

In the natal horoscope, Mid-Heaven (21 Scorpio), Ascendant (18 Capricorn), and Mars (17 Pisces) form a small triangle pattern. In addition, Neptune (7 Aquarius), Saturn (Gemini), and Moon (5 Leo) form another triangle pattern.

Moon Transits

Using your Ephemeris table or software program, specifically watch for those times in each monthly lunar cycle when Moon transits past:

- ✡ 21 Scorpio (natal Mid-Heaven)
- ✡ 18 Capricorn (natal Ascendant)
- ✡ 17 Pisces (natal Mars)
- ✡ 7 Aquarius (natal Neptune)
- ✡ 9 Gemini (natal Saturn)
- ✡ 5 Leo (natal Moon).

My research has shown that the times when Sun, and Mars pass these triangle corner points, pass the Mid-Heaven point, and pass the Ascendant point, deserve careful scrutiny.

Sun and Mars transits

For 2024:

- ✡ **Sun will pass 18 Capricorn on January 8, 7 Aquarius on January 27, 17 Pisces on March 7, 9 Gemini on May 30, 5 Leo on July 27, and 21 Scorpio on November 13.**
- ✡ **Mars will pass 18 Capricorn on January 29, 7 Aquarius on February 22, 17 Pisces on April 14, 9 Gemini on August 3, 5 Leo on November 23. Mars turns retrograde shortly after an does not progress any further.**

Declination

At the 2002 first trade date, Mars was at +22 degrees declination, and Venus was at -11 degrees declination. Moon was at its declination maxima.

For 2024:

- ☼ **Venus will be at its natal declination level for several days either side of February 26 and October 8.**

- ☼ **Mars will be at its natal declination level for several days either side of July 20.**

- ☼ **Moon will be at its declination maximum January 23, February 19, March 18, April 13, May 11, June 7, July 5, August 1, August 28, September 24, October 21, November 18, December 16.**

Australian Dollar

Australian dollar futures started trading on the Chicago Mercantile Exchange on January 13, 1987. As the horoscope in Figure 7-9 shows, Sun and Mercury are at Superior Conjunction at 23 degrees Capricorn.

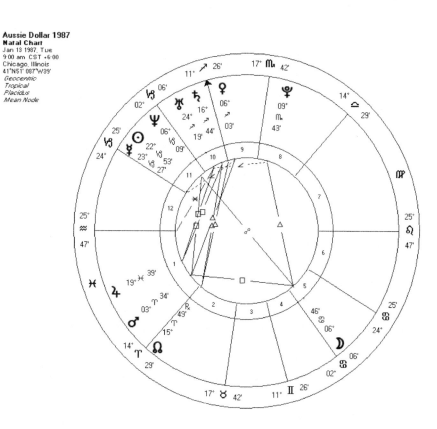

Figure 7-9
Australian Dollar First Trade Horoscope

In the natal horoscope, Neptune (6 Capricorn), Mars (3 Aries), and Moon (6 Cancer) form a right-angle triangle pattern. In addition, the Mid-Heaven is at 11 Sagittarius, and the Ascendant is at 25 Aquarius.

Moon Transits

Using your Ephemeris table or software program, specifically watch for those times in each monthly lunar cycle when Moon transits past:

- ☼ 6 Capricorn (natal Neptune)
- ☼ 3 Aries (natal Mars)
- ☼ 6 Cancer (natal Moon)
- ☼ 11 Sagittarius (natal Mid-Heaven)
- ☼ 25 Aquarius (natal Ascendant).

My research has further shown that the times when Sun and Mars each transit past these triangle corner points, the Mid-Heaven point, and the Ascendant point, all deserve careful scrutiny.

Sun and Mars transits

For 2024:

- ☼ **Sun will have just passed the natal Neptune location (6 Capricorn) at the start of the year. Sun will pass 25 Aquarius on February 14, 3 Aries on March 23, 6 Cancer on June 27, and 11 Sagittarius on December 2.**

- ☼ **Mars will pass 6 Capricorn on January 13. Mars will then pass 25 Aquarius on March 16, 3 Aries on May 5, and 6 Cancer on September 15. Mars turns retrograde shortly after an does not progress any further.**

Declination

At the January 13, 1987 first trade date, Venus was at 12 degrees declination and Mars was at 15 degrees declination. Moon was at its maximum declination.

For 2024:

○ **Venus will be at its natal declination level for several days either side of May 12, July 25, and December 22.**

○ **Mars will be at its natal declination level for several days either side of August 23.**

○ **Moon will be at its declination maximum January 23, February 19, March 18, April 13, May 11, June 7, July 5, August 1, August 28, September 24, October 21, November 18, and December 16.**

Mercury Retrograde

Currency traders should pay close attention to Mercury retrograde events as they can bear a good alignment to trend changes on the Australian Dollar.

For 2024, Mercury will be:

○ **retrograde from April 1 through April 24**

○ **retrograde from August 5 through August 27**

○ **retrograde from November 26 through December 14.**

Debt Instruments

30-Year Bond Futures

30-Year Bond futures started trading in Chicago on August 22, 1977. Figure 7-10 presents the first trade horoscope for this date.

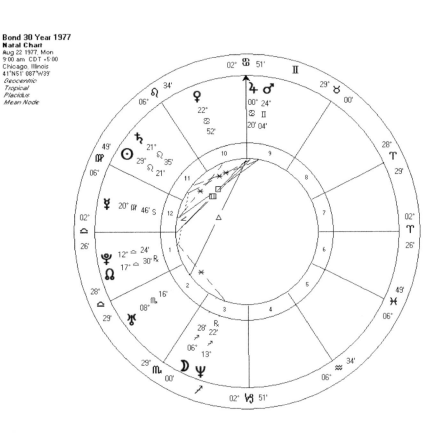

Figure 7-10
First Trade Horoscope for 30-Year Bond futures

In the natal horoscope, I am not seeing any distinct geometric shapes. Therefore, the best approach is to consider the Mid-Heaven (2 Cancer) and Ascendant (2 Libra) points.

Moon Transits

Using your Ephemeris table or software program, specifically watch for those times in each monthly lunar cycle when Moon transits past:

- ☿ 2 Cancer (natal Mid-Heaven)
- ☿ 2 Libra (natal Ascendant).

My research has further shown that the times when Sun and Mars each transit past these triangle corner points, the Mid-Heaven point, and the Ascendant point, all deserve careful scrutiny.

Sun and Mars transits

For 2024:

Sun will pass the natal Mid-Heaven at 2 Cancer on June 21. Sun will then pass the natal Ascendant on September 24.
Mars will pass the natal Mid-Heaven at 2 Cancer on September 8. Mars turns retrograde shortly after and does not progress any further.

Declination

At the August 22, 1977 first trade date Venus was at 17 degrees declination and Mars was at 16.5 degrees declination. Two significant planets both at the same declination level at the first trade date is more than just a little curious. Moon was within a fraction of a degree of being at its minimum declination.

For 2024,

- ☼ **Venus will be at its natal declination level for several days either side of May 26, and July 13.**

- ☼ **Mars will be at its natal declination level for several days either side of August 29.**

- ☼ **Moon will be at its minimum declination: January 10, February 6, March 5, April 1, April 28, May 25, June 22, July 19, August 16, September 12, October 9, November 5, December 3, and December 30.**

Mercury Retrograde

In the first trade horoscope in Figure 17-10 note that the position of Mercury (at 20 Virgo) is further delineated by a letter *S*. This letter denotes *stationary*. The term stationary refers to the day immediately prior to a planet turning retrograde and starting to move backwards in the zodiac wheel. This first trade date of August 22, 1977 comes one day prior to Mercury turning retrograde. Was this also a factor in selecting this first trade date?

For 2024, Mercury will be:

- ☼ **retrograde from April 1 through April 24**

- ☼ **retrograde from August 5 through August 27**

- ☼ **retrograde from November 26 through December 14.**

10-Year Treasury Note Futures

10-Year Treasury Notes started trading in Chicago on May 3, 1982. Figure 7-11 presents the first trade horoscope for this date.

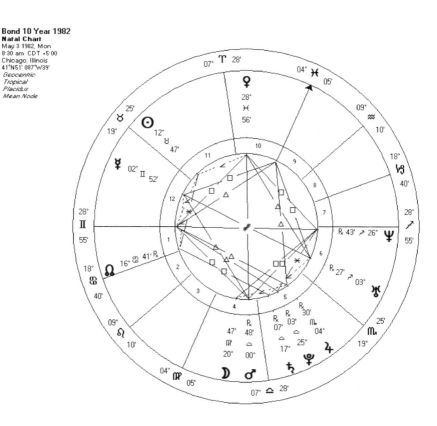

Figure 7-11
First Trade Horoscope for 10-Year Treasury Note futures

In the natal horoscope, there are two triangular shapes, both emanating from the Mid-Heaven point at 4 Pisces. One triangle comprises the Mid-Heaven (4 Pisces), Ascendant (28 Gemini), and Jupiter (4 Scorpio). The second triangle comprises the Mid-Heaven (4 Pisces), Mercury (2

Gemini), and Uranus (3 Sagittarius). Furthermore, there is a square pattern comprising Venus (28 Pisces), the Ascendant (28 Gemini), Mars (0 Libra), and Neptune (26 Sagittarius). This is all assuming a first trade start time of 8:30 a.m.

Moon Transits

Using your Ephemeris table or software program, specifically watch for those times in each monthly lunar cycle when Moon transits past:

- ☼ 4 Pisces (natal Mid-Heaven)
- ☼ 28 Gemini (natal Ascendant)
- ☼ 4 Scorpio (natal Jupiter)
- ☼ 2 Gemini (natal Mercury)
- ☼ 3 Sagittarius (natal Uranus)
- ☼ Venus (28 Pisces)
- ☼ Mars (0 Libra)
- ☼ Neptune (26 Sagittarius).

My research has shown that the times when Sun and Mars each transit past these triangle corner points, the Mid-Heaven point, and the Ascendant point, all deserve careful scrutiny.

Sun and Mars transits

For 2024:

Sun will pass the natal Mid-Heaven at 4 Pisces on February 23. Sun will then pass 28 Pisces on March 18, 2 Gemini on May 22, 28 Gemini on June 18, 0 Libra on September 22, 4 Scorpio on October 27, 3 Sagittarius on November 24, and 26 Sagittarius on December 17.

As the New Year starts, Mars will be passing the natal Neptune point (26 Sagittarius). Mars will pass 4 Pisces on March 28, 28 Pisces on April 28, 2 Gemini on July 23, and 28 Gemini on September 1. Mars turns retrograde shortly after and does not progress any further.

Declination

At the May 3, 1982 first trade date Venus was at -24 degrees declination and Mars was at -9 degrees declination.

For 2024:

- ☼ **Venus will be at its natal declination level for several days either side of February 27, and October 9.**

- ☼ **Mars will be at its natal declination level for several days either side of May 15.**

Retrograde

Note that in this first trade horoscope Mars is denoted *Rx* which stands for *retrograde*. Therein rests another valuable clue as to the selection of the first trade date.

- ☼ **In 2024, Mars will turn retrograde on December 6 and will remain so until February 23, 2025.**

Mercury retrograde events also bear watching when following price action on the 10-Year Treasury Notes.

For 2024, Mercury will be:

- ☼ **retrograde from April 1 through April 24**

- ☼ **retrograde from August 5 through August 27**

- ☼ **retrograde from November 26 through December 14.**

Grains, Fiber, and Wood

Wheat, Corn, and Oats

1877 Futures

Wheat, Corn, and Oats futures all share the same first trade date of January 2, 1877. The horoscope in Figure 7-12 shows planetary placements at that date.

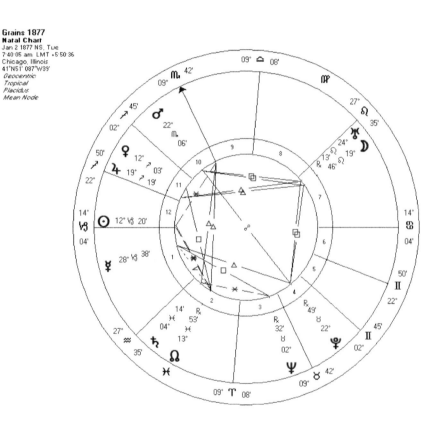

Figure 7-12
First Trade Horoscope for Wheat, Corn, and Oats futures

Assuming a 7:40 a.m. first trade start time, in the natal horoscope there is a triangular shape evident. However, one of its corners is Pluto (22 Taurus). Pluto had not yet been discovered in 1877, so this geometric pattern is moot. The Mid-Heaven in this 1877 horoscope is at 9 Scorpio and the Ascendant is at 14 Capricorn. Given the historical gravitas of 14 Cancer, the choice of this first trade date with an ascendant point 180-degress opposite to 14 Cancer is not a random occurrence.

Moon Transits

Using your Ephemeris table or software program, specifically watch for those times in each monthly lunar cycle when Moon transits past:

- ☿ **9 Scorpio (natal Mid-Heaven)**
- ☿ **14 Capricorn (natal Ascendant).**

Declination

At the January 2, 1877 first trade date Venus was at -8 degrees declination and Mars was at -8 degrees declination. Two significant planets at the same declination level is surely not an accidental occurrence. In addition, Moon was within a couple degrees of being at its declination maximum.

In 2022, Venus was at its natal declination for several days either side of March 10. This time frame delivered a price spike on Wheat in response to the Russian invasion of Ukraine. June 6 marked another transit of Venus past its natal declination. This event started a significant price drawdown in Wheat prices. Other natal declination transits through 2022 and 2023 all aligned to price moves–some modest, some larger.

For 2024:

○ **Venus will be at its natal declination point for several days either side of January 14, April 10, August 23, and November 22.**

○ **Mars will be at its natal declination point for several days on either side of May 19, 2024.**

○ **Moon will be at its declination maximum January 23, February 19, March 18, April 13, May 11, June 7, July 5, August 1, August 28, September 24, October 21, November 18, and December 16.**

Chicago Board of Trade (CBOT) 1848

W.D. Gann was known to follow a first trade horoscope wheel from April 3, 1848, the date the Chicago Board of Trade (CBOT) was founded. Figure 7-13 shows this horoscope wheel.

In the 1877 Wheat/Corn natal horoscope, the Sun is at 12 Capricorn, exactly square to the location of Sun in the 1848 horoscope.

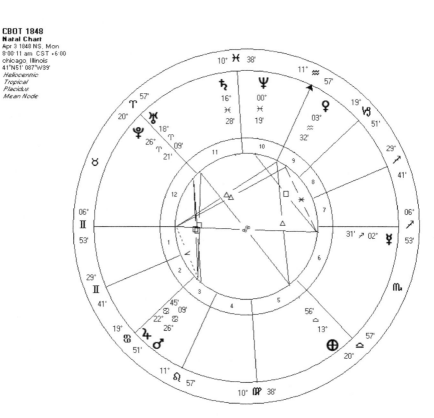

Figure 7-13
1848 First Trade Horoscope for CBOT

The 1848 CBOT chart has no distinct geometric patterns in it. The Mid-Heaven in this 1848 horoscope is at 11 Aquarius and the Ascendant is at 6 Gemini.

Moon Transits

Using your Ephemeris table or software program, specifically watch for those times in each monthly lunar cycle when Moon transits past:

- ☼ 11 Aquarius (natal Mid-Heaven)
- ☼ 6 Gemini (natal Ascendant).

Declination

At the April 3, 1848 first trade date Venus was at -22 degrees declination and Mars was at +22 degrees declination. These two planets are contra-parallel in declination. The choice of this first trade date was definitely no accident. In addition, Moon was at 0 degrees of declination.

In 2023, Venus was at its natal declination for several days either side of July 1 and August 1. A look at the price chart of Wheat reveals sizeable price moves in the immediate time around these dates.

For 2024:

- ☼ **Venus will be at its natal declination point for several days either side of February 11, March 13, September 23, and October 26.**

- ☼ **Mars will be at its natal declination point for several days on either side of October 9, 2024.**

- ☼ **Moon will be at 0-degrees declination on January 3, 16 and 30, February 13, March 11, April 7, May 4, June 1 and 28, July 12 and 25, August 8 and 21, September 4 and 18, October 1, 16 and 29, November 11, and December 22.**

Mercury Retrograde

Mercury retrograde events also bear watching when following price action on Wheat, Corn, and Oats.

For 2024, Mercury will be:

- ☼ **retrograde from April 1 through April 24**
- ☼ **retrograde from August 5 through August 27**
- ☼ **retrograde from November 26 through December 14.**

Soybeans

Soybean futures started trading in Chicago on October 5, 1936. The horoscope in Figure 7-14 illustrates the planetary placements at that time. Notice that Sun is exactly 90-degrees to the location of the Sun in the first trade horoscope for Wheat, Corn and Oats. Notice that Sun is 180-degrees from the Sun in the 1848 CBOT natal chart.

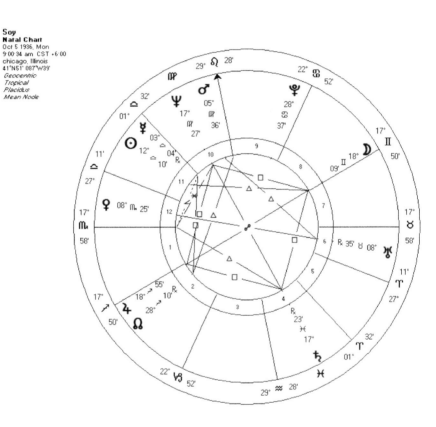

Figure 7-14
Soybean futures First Trade Horoscope

The regulatory officials who determined these first trade dates knew more about astrology than we may think. Studying the 1877 natal horoscope for Corn and Wheat reveals a further similarity to the 1936 Soybeans horoscope–Jupiter is at 18-19 degrees Sagittarius in both horoscopes.

The 1936 Soybeans horoscope chart has as square geometric pattern in it. This pattern comprises Moon (16 Gemini), Neptune (17 Virgo), Jupiter (18 Sagittarius), and Saturn (17 Pisces). The Mid-Heaven in this horoscope is at 14 Cancer and the Ascendant is at 12 Libra.

Moon Transits

Using your Ephemeris table or software program, specifically watch for those times in each monthly lunar cycle when Moon transits past:

- ✪ 17 Pisces (natal Saturn)
- ✪ 16 Gemini (natal Moon)
- ✪ 14 Cancer (natal Mid-Heaven)
- ✪ 17 Virgo (natal Neptune)
- ✪ 12 Libra (natal Ascendant)
- ✪ 18 Sagittarius (natal Jupiter).

My research has shown that the times when Sun, and Mars pass these corner points, the Mid-Heaven point, and the Ascendant point deserve careful scrutiny.

Sun and Mars transits

For 2024:

- ✪ **Sun will pass the natal Saturn at 17 Pisces on March 7. Sun will then pass 16 Gemini on June 6, 14 Cancer on July 5,**

17 Virgo on September 9, 12 Libra on October 4, and 18 Sagittarius on December 9.

☼ As the New Year starts, Mars will have just finished passing the natal Jupiter point (18 Sagittarius). Mars will then pass the natal Saturn at 17 Pisces on March 7, 16 Gemini on August 14, 17 Virgo on September 9, and 14 Cancer on September 29.

Declination

At the October 5, 1936 first trade date Venus was at -22 degrees declination and Mars was at +18 degrees declination. Moon was at its declination maximum.

In 2023, Venus was at its natal declination for several days either side of July 1 and August 1. A look at the price chart of Soybeans reveals a spiked double top pattern.

For 2024:

☼ **Venus will be at its natal declination point for several days either side of February 11, March 13, September 23, and October 26.**

☼ **Mars will be at its natal declination point for several days on either side of July 15, 2024.**

☼ **Moon will be at its declination maximum January 23, February 19, March 18, April 13, May 11, June 7, July 5, August 1, August 28, September 24, October 21, November 18, and December 16.**

Mercury Retrograde

Mercury retrograde events also bear watching when following price action on Soybeans.

For 2024, Mercury will be:

- ☼ **retrograde from April 1 through April 24**
- ☼ **retrograde from August 5 through August 27**
- ☼ **retrograde from November 26 through December 14.**

Cotton

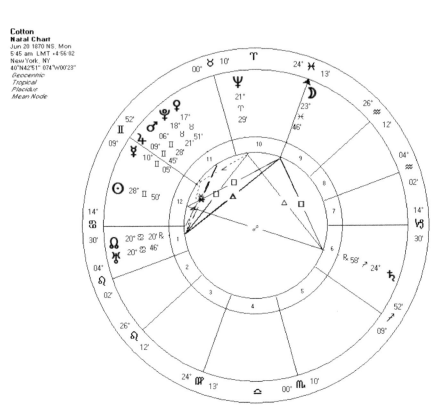

Figure 7-15
Cotton futures First Trade Horoscope

After sifting through back editions of New York newspapers, I concluded that Cotton futures first started trading on June 20, 1870. The horoscope wheel in Figure 7-15 illustrates planetary placements at that time. An early first trade time of 5:45 a.m. is assumed. Using this early hour of the morning, the Moon is at the same degree and sign location (24 Pisces) as is the Mid-Heaven in the New York Stock Exchange natal horoscope wheel from 1792. Furthermore, Mars, Jupiter and Mercury are clustered around the location of 9 Gemini (which is where one finds Uranus in the USA 1776 natal chart). This horoscope wheel becomes even more intriguing when one considers that the date for the Cotton futures first trade was on the cusp of the Summer Solstice. And, with a first trade transaction of 5:45 a.m., the Mid-Heaven aligns to 24 Pisces and the Ascendant to 14 Cancer. Surely the selection of this June 20th first trade date is no accident.

The 1870 Cotton horoscope chart has as triangular geometric pattern in it. This pattern comprises Sun (28 Gemini), Saturn (24 Sagittarius), and Moon at 23 Pisces. The Mid-Heaven in this horoscope is at 24 Pisces, and the Ascendant is at 14 Cancer.

Moon Transits

Using your Ephemeris table or software program, specifically watch for those times in each monthly lunar cycle when Moon transits past:

- ✪ 23 Pisces (natal Moon and natal Mid-Heaven)
- ✪ 28 Gemini (natal Sun)
- ✪ 24 Sagittarius (natal Saturn)
- ✪ 14 Cancer (natal Ascendant).

My research has shown that the times when Sun and Mars each transit past these triangle corner points, the Mid-Heaven point, and the Ascendant point, deserve careful scrutiny.

Sun and Mars transits

For 2024:

- ✪ **Sun will pass the natal Mid-Heaven at 23 Pisces on March 13, 28 Gemini on June 18, 14 of Cancer on July 5, and 24 Sagittarius on December 15.**

☼ **As the New Year starts, Mars will have just finished passing the natal Saturn point (24 Sagittarius). Mars will then pass the natal Mid-Heaven at 23 Pisces on April 21, 24 Sagittarius on September 2, and 14 Cancer on September 29.**

Declination

At the June 20, 1870 first trade date Venus was at -10 degrees declination and Mars was at +18 degrees declination. Moon was within a degree of being at 0-degrees declination.

In 2023, Venus was at its natal declination for several days either side of January 14 and June 4. A look at the price chart of cotton reveals a profitable price reaction at both events. In 2022, Mars was at its natal declination for several days either side of October 22. This timeframe aligns to a significant price low for cotton at 72 cents per pound.

For 2024:

☼ **Venus will be at its natal declination point for several day either side of January 16, April 7, August 28, and November 17.**

☼ **Mars will be at its natal declination point for several days on either side of September 9, 2024.**

☼ **Moon will be at 0-degrees declination on January 3, 16 and 30, February 13, March 11, April 7, May 4, June 1 and 28, July 12 and 25, August 8 and 21, September 4 and 18, October 1, 16 and 29, November 11, and December 22.**

Lumber

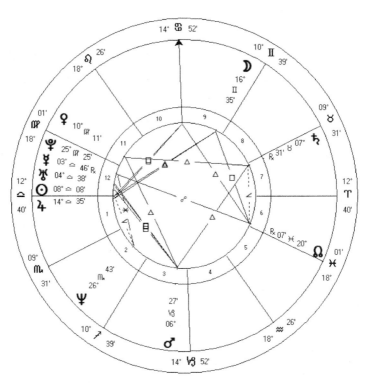

Lumber 1969
Natal Chart
Oct 1 1969 NS, Wed
7:15 am CDT +5:00
Chicago, Illinois
41°N51' 087°W39'
Geocentric
Tropical
Placidus
Mean Node

Figure 7-16
Lumber futures First Trade Horoscope

Lumber futures started trading in Chicago on October 1, 1969. The horoscope in Figure 7-16 shows planetary placements at the first trade date. Assuming a 7:15 a.m. first trade transaction, the Mid-Heaven point is at 14 degrees of Cancer.

The 1969 Lumber futures horoscope chart has as triangular geometric pattern in it. This pattern comprises Saturn (7 Taurus), Venus (10

Virgo), and Mars (6 Capricorn). The Ascendant is at 12 Cancer. Moon is at 16 Gemini.

Moon Transits

Using your Ephemeris table or software program, specifically watch for those times in each monthly lunar cycle when Moon transits past:

- ☼ 16 Gemini (natal Moon)
- ☼ 8 to 14 Libra (natal Sun, natal Ascendant, natal Jupiter)
- ☼ 7 Taurus (natal Saturn)
- ☼ 14 Cancer (natal Mid-Heaven)
- ☼ 10 Virgo (natal Venus)
- ☼ 6 Capricorn (natal Mars).

My research has shown that the times when Sun and Mars transit past these triangle corner points, the Mid-Heaven point, and the Ascendant point, all deserve careful scrutiny.

Sun and Mars transits

For 2024:

- ☼ **Sun will pass the natal Mid-Heaven at 23 Pisces on March 13, 28 Gemini on June 18, 14 of Cancer on July 5, and 24 Sagittarius on December 15.**
- ☼ **As the New Year starts, Mars will have just finished passing the natal Saturn point (24 Sagittarius). Mars will then pass the natal Mid-Heaven at 23 Pisces on April 21, 24 Sagittarius on September 2, and 14 Cancer on September 29.**

Mercury Retrograde

The most illuminating feature of this first trade horoscope is the fact that Mercury was retrograde. If trading Lumber futures holds appeal for you, pay close attention to Mercury retrograde events as they may well align to price swing points.

For example, in May 2021, Lumber prices made headline news when they reached an unprecedented price level of $1400 per thousand board feet. Within two weeks of this peak, Mercury turned retrograde and with that a swift price drawdown began. Mercury was retrograde from January 13 to February 3, 2022. During this event, Lumber futures prices fell from $1200 to $826 per thousand board feet. A few days prior to the start of another retrograde on May 10, 2022, Lumber futures prices again started to fall.

For 2024, Mercury will be:

- ☼ **retrograde from April 1 through April 24**
- ☼ **retrograde from August 5 through August 27**
- ☼ **retrograde from November 26 through December 14.**

Declination

At the 1969 first trade date, Mars was at -15 degrees declination, Venus was at +22 degrees declination, and Moon was at its declination maximum. Looking back at the historically significant price high in May 2021 shows that Venus was at its natal declination level. In early March 2022 at another dramatic price high, Mars was at 0-degrees declination. I take this as more than just a little curious.

For 2024:

- ☼ Venus will be at its natal declination level for several days either side of June 4 and July 3.

- ☼ Mars will be at its natal declination for several days either side of April 19.

- ☼ Moon will be at its declination maximum January 23, February 19, March 18, April 13, May 11, June 7, July 5, August 1, August 28, September 24, October 21, November 18, and December 16.

Energy

Crude Oil

West Texas Intermediate Crude Oil futures started trading for the first time in New York on March 30, 1983. A unique alignment of celestial points can be seen in the horoscope in Figure 7-17.

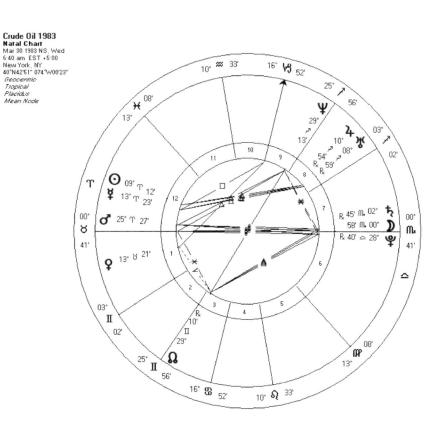

Figure 7-17
Crude Oil futures First Trade Horoscope

This is assuming a first trade start time of 6:40 a.m. Notice how Mars (1 Taurus), North Node (29 Gemini), Saturn/Pluto/Moon (2 Scorpio), and Neptune (29 Sagittarius) conspire to form a rectangle. The Mid-Heaven point is 17 of Capricorn. Mars is at the Ascendant point.

Oil can be a complex instrument to analyze using astrology. Given the peculiar rectangular shape that appears in the horoscope, one strategy for analyzing Oil futures prices is to use natal transits with a focus on transiting Sun and transiting Mars making 0-degree aspects to the four corner points of the rectangle. My research has shown that the tenor of the price reaction as Sun and Mars each pass the various corner points varies from year to year.

In 2023, the four corners of the peculiar rectangle were passed by as follows:

- ⚙ Sun passed 0-degrees to the natal Mars location from April 9 through April 22. This marked the start of a decline that saw Oil prices give up over $20 per barrel.

- ⚙ Sun passed 0-degrees to the natal Node location from June 7 through June 22. Price traded within a volatile range of $10 per barrel.

- ⚙ Sun passed 0-degrees to the natal (Saturn/Pluto/Moon) location from October 18 through November 1.

- ⚙ Sun passed 0-degrees to the natal Neptune location from December 14 through the end of the year.

- ⚙ Mars passed the natal Node location from March 19 to April 2. This period saw Oil rally nearly $20 per barrel in price to reach the $83 per barrel level.

- ⚙ Mars passed 0-degrees to the natal (Saturn/Pluto/Moon) location from October 10 through 20. As Mars began its transit, Oil prices had been falling. Not only did Mars arrest this decline, hostilities between Israel and Hamas terrorists erupted, sending Oil traders scrambling to take long positions.

For 2024:

- ✿ **Sun will pass the natal Neptune point in the first week of January**

- ✿ **Sun will pass the natal Mars point from April 9 through April 22**

- ✿ **Sun will pass 0-degrees to the natal Node location from June 7 through June 22**

- ✿ **Sun will pass 0-degrees to the natal (Saturn/Pluto/Moon) location from October 18 through November 1.**

- ✿ **Sun will pass 0-degrees to the natal Neptune location from December 14 through the end of the year.**

- ✿ **Mars will pass the natal Mid-Heaven several days either side of January 27**

- ✿ **Mars will pass the natal Mars location several days either side of June 8**

- ✿ **Mars will pass the natal Node location several days either side of September 7.**

Retrograde

Crude Oil is influenced by Mercury retrograde and Venus retrograde.

For 2024, Mercury will be:

- ✿ **retrograde from April 1 through April 24**

- ✿ **retrograde from August 5 through August 27**

- ✿ **retrograde from November 26 through December 14.**

For 2024, Venus will not be retrograde.

Declination

At the 1983 first trade date, Venus was at its maximum declination of +24 degrees. This feature along with the peculiar rectangle geometric shape in the horoscope wheel suggest that this first trade date was not just a random selection.

An examination of past events where Venus was passing +24 degrees of declination shows a correlation to price moves up and down on Oil. One curious observation that does stand out dates to April 2020 when for a brief couple trading sessions, Oil futures traded negative. Venus just so happened to be at 0-degrees declination at that time.

For 2024,

- ☿ **Venus will be at its declination maximum around June 18**

- ☿ **Moon will be at 0-degrees declination on January 3, 16 and 30, February 13, March 11, April 7, May 4, June 1 and 28, July 12 and 25, August 8 and 21, September 4 and 18, October 1, 16 and 29, November 11, and December 22.**

Natural Gas

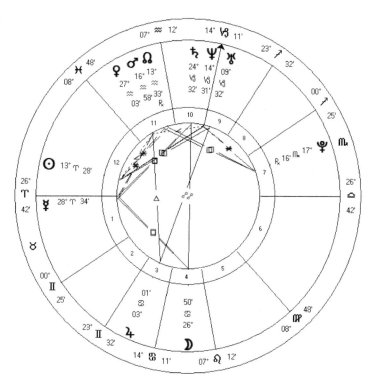

Figure 7-18
Natural Gas futures First Trade Horoscope

Natural Gas futures started trading in Chicago on April 3, 1990. At that date, Moon was withing a degree of its declination maximum. Mars was at its declination minimum. Venus was at -19 degrees declination. Moon and Mars both at their declination extremes suggests this first trade date was not a random selection.

The 1990 Natural Gas horoscope chart has a triangular geometric pattern embedded in it with corner points of Moon, Saturn, and Mid-Heaven. Moreover, the Mid-Heaven is at 13 Capricorn and within orb of being 90-degrees square to the ever-mysterious 14 of Cancer point. The Ascendant is at 24 Aries.

Moon Transits

Using your Ephemeris table or software program, specifically watch for those times in each monthly lunar cycle when Moon transits past:

- ☼ 13 Capricorn (natal Mid-Heaven)
- ☼ 26 Aries (natal Ascendant)
- ☼ 26 Cancer (natal Moon)
- ☼ 24 Capricorn (natal Saturn)

My research has shown that the times when Sun and Mars each transit past these triangle corner points, the Mid-Heaven point, and the Ascendant point, all deserve careful scrutiny.

Sun and Mars transits

For 2024:

- ☼ **Sun will pass the natal Mid-Heaven at 13 Capricorn on January 5. Mars will follow close behind on January 23.**
- ☼ **Sun will pass 26 Aries on April 15. Mars will follow on June 4.**
- ☼ **Sun will pass the natal Saturn point at 24 Capricorn on January 14. Mars will follow on February 5.**

Declination

In 2024:

☼ **Venus will be at -19 degrees declination for several days either side of February 3, March 22, September 14, and November 1.**

☼ **Mars will be at its declination minimum for several days either side of January 26**

☼ **Moon will be at its declination maximum January 23, February 19, March 18, April 13, May 11, June 7, July 5, August 1, August 28, September 24, October 21, November 18, and December 16.**

Softs

Coffee

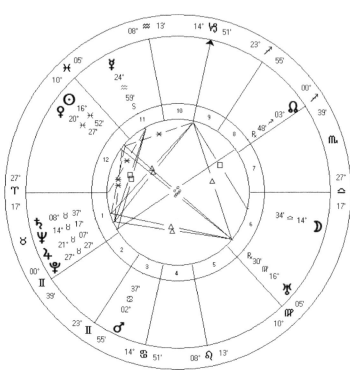

Figure 7-19
Coffee futures First Trade Horoscope

Coffee futures started trading in New York in early March of 1882. The horoscope wheel in Figure 7-19 illustrates planetary placements at that time.

The 1882 Coffee horoscope chart has a kite-shaped geometric pattern in it. The points of this triangle are: 14 Capricorn (Mid-Heaven), 16 Pisces, 14 Taurus (Neptune), and 16 Virgo (Uranus). The Ascendant is at 27 Aries. This is assuming an 8:00 a.m. first trade start time.

Moon Transits

Using your Ephemeris table or software program, specifically watch for those times in each monthly lunar cycle when Moon transits past:

- ✪ 14 Taurus (natal Neptune)
- ✪ 16 Virgo (natal Uranus)
- ✪ 14 Capricorn (natal Mid-Heaven)
- ✪ 16 Pisces (natal Sun)
- ✪ 27 Aries (natal Ascendant).

My research has shown that the times when Sun and Mars each transit past these triangle corner points, the Mid-Heaven point, and the Ascendant point, all deserve careful scrutiny.

Sun and Mars transits

For 2024:

- ✪ **Sun will pass the natal Mid-Heaven at 14 Capricorn on January 5. Mars will follow close behind on April 12.**
- ✪ **Sun will pass 27 Aries on April 16. Mars will follow on June 5.**
- ✪ **Sun will pass 14 Taurus on May 3. Mars will follow on June 28.**
- ✪ **Sun will pass 16 Virgo on September 8.**

Declination

In early March 1882, Mars was +20 degrees declination and Venus was at -7 degrees. Moon was at 0-degrees of declination.

In 2024:

- ☼ **Mars will be at +20 degrees declination for several days either side of September 25.**

- ☼ **Venus will be at -7 degrees declination for a couple days either side of January 12, April 12, August 23, and November 23.**

- ☼ **Moon will be at 0-degrees declination on January 3, 16 and 30, February 13, March 11, April 7, May 4, June 1 and 28, July 12 and 25, August 8 and 21, September 4 and 18, October 1, 16 and 29, November 11, and December 22.**

Sugar

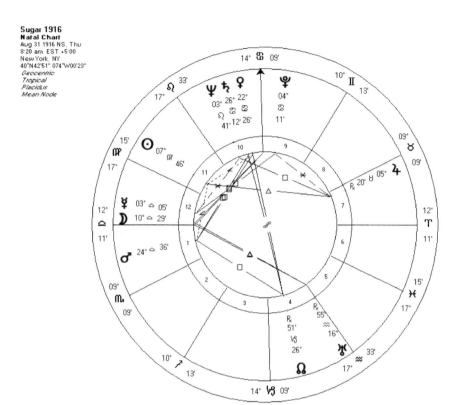

Figure 7-20
Sugar futures First Trade Horoscope

Sugar as a bulk commodity started trading in New York as early as 1881. Old editions of New York newspapers suggest that, in September 1914, there were plans to open a formal Sugar Exchange, but these plans were scuttled by World War I. Part-way through the war, a formal Exchange *did* open on August 31, 1916. The horoscope wheel in Figure 7-20 illustrates planetary placements at that time. What stands out on this chart wheel is the triangle formation with Mars at its apex. As well, the

Mid-Heaven (MH) is at 14 of Cancer if one assumes that the very first trade was conducted at 8:20 a.m.

Moon Transits

Using your Ephemeris table or software program, specifically watch for those times in each monthly lunar cycle when Moon transits past

- ☼ 14 Cancer (natal Mid-Heaven)
- ☼ 26 Cancer (natal Saturn)
- ☼ 12 Libra (natal Ascendant)
- ☼ 24 Libra (natal Mars)
- ☼ 26 Capricorn (natal Node).

My research has shown that the times when Sun and Mars each transit past these triangle corner points, the Mid-Heaven point, and the Ascendant point, all deserve careful scrutiny.

Sun and Mars transits

For 2024:

- ☼ **Sun will pass 26 Capricorn on January 16. Mars will follow on February 7.**
- ☼ **Sun will pass 14 Cancer on July 5 and 26 Cancer on July 19. Mars will follow suit on September 29, and October 27 respectively.**
- ☼ **Sun will pass 12 Libra on October 4 and 24 Libra on October 16.**

Declination

At the August 31, 1916 first trade date, Venus was at +18 degrees declination and Mars was at -9 degrees declination. Moon was within a whisker of being at 0-degrees of declination. A look back at past price data for Sugar prices shows that this connection still aligns to price inflection points. For example, in mid-September 2023, Mars was passing through -9 degrees of declination as Sugar futures price made an interim swing high and proceeded to decline by 1 cent per pound ($1100 per contract).

In 2024:

- ☼ **Venus will be at +2 degrees declination for several days either side of April 27 and August 9.**

- ☼ **Mars will be at -9 degrees declination for several days either side of April 4.**

- ☼ **Moon will be at 0-degrees declination on January 3, 16, and 30, February 13, March 11, April 7, May 4, June 1 and 28, July 12 and 25, August 8 and 21, September 4 and 18, October 1, 16 and 29, November 11, and December 22.**

Mercury Retrograde

Mercury retrograde events have a propensity to align to short-term trend changes on Sugar price.

For 2024, Mercury will be:

- ☼ **retrograde from April 1 through April 24**

- ☼ **retrograde from August 5 through August 27**

- ☼ **retrograde from November 26 through December 14.**

Cocoa

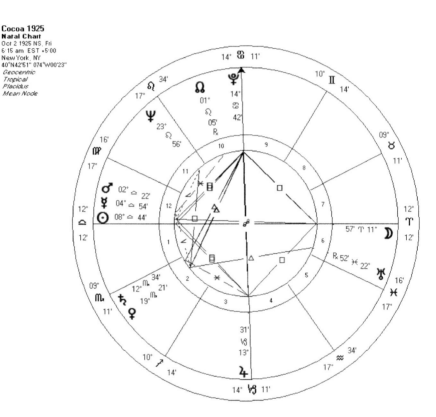

Figure 7-21
Cocoa futures First Trade Horoscope

Cocoa futures started trading in New York in early October 1925. The horoscope in Figure 7-21 shows planetary placements at the first trade date. What I find peculiar on this horoscope wheel is the Mid-Heaven point located at 14 of Cancer, that same mysterious point that appears in the First Trade horoscope of the New York Stock Exchange. There is also a square-shaped pattern evident in this horoscope. The points of the square are: Mid-Heaven (14 Cancer), Ascendant (12 Libra), Jupiter (13 Capricorn), and Moon (11 Aries).

Moon Transits

Using your Ephemeris table or software program, specifically watch for those times in each monthly lunar cycle when Moon transits past

- ✦ 14 Cancer (natal Mid-Heaven)
- ✦ 12 Libra (natal Ascendant)
- ✦ 13 Capricorn (natal Jupiter)
- ✦ 11 Aries (natal Moon).

My research has shown that the times when Sun and Mars each transit past these triangle corner points, the Mid-Heaven point, and the Ascendant point, all deserve careful scrutiny.

Sun and Mars transits

For 2024:

- ✦ **Sun will pass 13 Capricorn on January 3. Mars will follow close behind on January 21.**
- ✦ **Sun will pass 11 Aries on March 31. Mars will follow closely on May 14.**
- ✦ **Sun will pass the natal Mid-Heaven at 14 Cancer on July 5. Mars will pass 14 Cancer on September 29.**
- ✦ **Sun will pass 12 Libra on October 4.**

Declination

In early October 1925 at the first trade date, Mars was +1 degree declination and Venus was -23 degrees (minimum). Moon was at its declination maximum. As an example of the correlation between declination and price, consider that in mid-July 2023 Cocoa futures price exhibited a swing low and proceeded to gain $170 per metric tonne ($1700 per contract). This price rally lost momentum in late July when Mars passed through +1 degrees of declination.

In 2024:

- ☼ **Venus will be at -23 degrees declination for several days either side of February 26, and October 8.**

- ☼ **Mars will be at +1 degree of declination for several days either side of June 25.**

- ☼ **Moon will be at its declination maximum January 23, February 19, March 18, April 13, May 11, June 7, July 5, August 1, August 28, September 24, October 21, November 18, and December 16.**

Mercury Retrograde

Mercury retrograde events have a propensity to align to short-term trend changes on Cocoa futures prices.

For 2024, Mercury will be:

- ☼ **retrograde from April 1 through April 24**

- ☼ **retrograde from August 5 through August 27**

- ☼ **retrograde from November 26 through December 14.**

Conjunctions and Elongations

The 1925 natal horoscope shows Sun and Mercury conjunct (0-degrees apart). My research has shown that events of Mercury being at its maximum easterly and westerly elongations, and events of Mercury being at its inferior and superior conjunctions align quite well to pivot swing points.

The price chart in Figure 7-22 illustrates some easterly and westerly elongation events that occurred in the first nine months of 2023. The alignment to pivot price points, while not perfectly exact, is intriguing and deserving of attention.

Figure 7-22
Cocoa price and Mercury elongation events

For 2024:

- ☼ **Mercury will be at its greatest easterly elongation March 24, July 22, and November 16.**

- ☼ **For 2024, Mercury will be at its greatest westerly elongation January 12, May 9, September 4, and December 24.**

Meats

Feeder Cattle

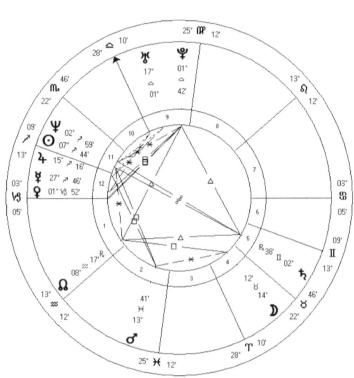

Figure 7-23
Feeder Cattle First Trade Horoscope

Feeder Cattle futures started trading in Chicago on November 30, 1971. The horoscope in Figure 7-23 shows planetary placements at the first trade date.

Looking carefully at the placements, one can see that Pluto (1 Libra), Saturn (2 Gemini), and Node (8 Aquarius) form a triangular pattern. In addition, the Mid-Heaven is at 28 Libra and the Ascendant is at 3 Capricorn.

Moon Transits

Using your Ephemeris table or software program, specifically watch for those times in each monthly lunar cycle when Moon transits past:

- ☼ 3 Capricorn (natal Ascendant)
- ☼ 8 Aquarius (natal Node)
- ☼ 2 Gemini (natal Saturn)
- ☼ 1 Libra (natal Pluto)
- ☼ 28 Libra (natal Mid-Heaven).

My research has shown that the times when Sun and Mars each transit past these triangle corner points, the Mid-Heaven point, and the Ascendant point, all deserve careful scrutiny.

Sun and Mars transits

To illustrate the correlation between Feeder cattle price volatility and Sun passing thee key points, consider that in late May 2023, Feeder cattle prices surged higher. The trigger that started the move–Sun passing the 2 of Gemini point.

For 2024:

- ☼ **Mars will pass 2 Capricorn on January 7.**
- ☼ **Sun will pass 8 Aquarius on January 28. Mars will pass 8 Aquarius on February 23.**

- ☼ **Sun will pass 2 Gemini on May 22. Mars will follow on July 24.**

- ☼ **Sun will pass 1 Libra on September 23 and 27 Libra on October 20. Sun will pass 2 Capricorn on December 23.**

Declination

At the 1971 first trade date, Venus was at -22 degrees declination. Mars was at 9 degrees declination. As an example of the correlation between declination and price, consider that in July 2023 Feeder cattle prices reached a significant high of $250 per hundred weight. This occurred just as Venus was at -22 degrees declination.

For 2024:

- ☼ **Venus will be at -22 degrees declination for several days either side of February 9, March 14, September 21, and October 24.**

- ☼ **Mars will be at 9 degrees declination around July 29.**

Live Cattle

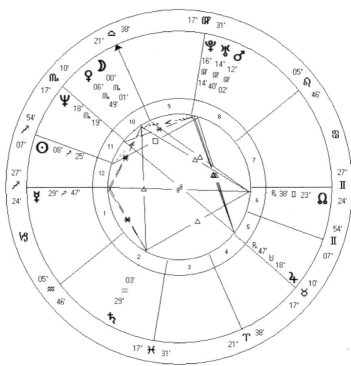

Live Cattle Futures
Natal Chart
Nov 30 1964, Mon
8:32:38 am CST •6:00
chicago, Illinois
41°N51' 087°W39'
Geocentric
Tropical
Placidus
Mean Node

Figure 7-24
Live Cattle futures First Trade Horoscope

Live Cattle futures started trading in Chicago on November 30, 1964. The horoscope in Figure 7-24 shows planetary placements at the first trade date.

Looking carefully at the placements, one can see that the Mid-Heaven/Moon (0 Scorpio), Saturn (29 Aquarius), and Node (23 Gemini) form a triangular pattern. In addition, the Ascendant is at 3 Capricorn.

Given the relation between Feeder cattle and Live cattle, I find it curiously interesting how the Mid-Heaven for each contract is practically at the same degree point in the sign of Libra.

Moon Transits

Using your Ephemeris table or software program, specifically watch for those times in each monthly lunar cycle when Moon transits past:

- ☼ 2 Capricorn (natal Ascendant)
- ☼ 23 Gemini (natal Node)
- ☼ 0 Scorpio (natal Moon/natal Mid-Heaven).

My research has shown that the times when Sun and Mars each transit past these triangle corner points, the Mid-Heaven point, and the Ascendant point, all deserve careful scrutiny.

Sun and Mars transits

To illustrate the correlation between Live cattle price volatility and Sun or Mars passing these key points, consider that in late March 2023, Live cattle prices rallied higher. The trigger–Mars passing the 23 Gemini point.

For 2024:

- ☼ **Mars will pass 3 Capricorn on January 9.**
- ☼ **Sun will pass 29 Aquarius on February 18.**
- ☼ **Mars will pass 29 Aquarius on March 22.**
- ☼ **Sun will pass 23 Gemini on June 13. Mars will follow on August 24.**
- ☼ **Sun will pass 0 Scorpio on October 23 and 3 Capricorn on December 24.**

Declination

At the 1964 first trade date, Venus was at 6 degrees declination. Mars was at 20 degrees declination. As an example of the correlation between declination and price, consider that in late March 2023 Mars was passing through 20 degrees of declination. Live cattle futures prices commenced a rally that saw price gain 14 cents per pound ($5600 per contract).

For 2024:

☼ **Venus will be at 6 degrees declination for several days either side of May 5, August 2, and December 11.**

☼ **Mars will be at 20 degrees declination around September 21.**

Lean Hogs

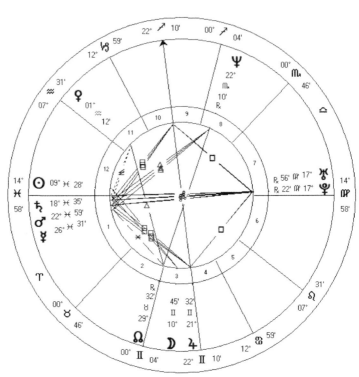

Figure 7-25
Lean Hogs futures First Trade Horoscope

Lean Hog futures started trading in Chicago on February 28, 1966. The horoscope in Figure 7-25 shows planetary placements at the first trade date assuming a 6:45 a.m. start of trading. The most illuminating feature of this horoscope is the appearance of a large square pattern (assuming a 6:45 a.m. trade start) with corners at Ascendant (14 Pisces), Jupiter (21 Gemini), Pluto (17 Virgo), and the Mid-Heaven (22 Sagittarius).

Moon Transits

Using your Ephemeris table or software program, specifically watch for those times in each monthly lunar cycle when Moon transits past:

- ✿ 14 Pisces (natal Ascendant)
- ✿ 21 Gemini (natal Jupiter)
- ✿ 17 Virgo (natal Pluto)
- ✿ 22 Sagittarius (natal Mid-Heaven)
- ✿ 9 to 14 Pisces (natal Sun and Ascendant)

My research has shown that the times when Sun and Mars each transit past these triangle corner points, the Mid-Heaven point, and the Ascendant point, all deserve careful scrutiny.

Sun and Mars transits

Lean hogs are notorious for their price volatility. There are only a handful of meat processors in North America that handle hogs. These players control the futures market. Hence the unpredictable volatility.

For 2024:

- ✿ **Sun will be at 14 Pisces on March 4. Mars will follow on Apil 10.**
- ✿ **Sun will be at 21 Gemini on June 11. Mars will pass 21 Gemini on August 21.**
- ✿ **Sun will pass 17 Virgo on September 9.**

Declination

At the 1966 first trade date, Venus was at 2 degrees declination. Mars was at 1 degree of declination. Moon was very nearly at its maximum declination. Two significant planets practically at the same declination while Moon is nearly at its declination max suggests this first trade date was not a random selection.

In late February 2022, Lean hogs price recorded an interim top. This came just as Venus was at nearing 4 degrees of declination. In early August 2022, Mars at 2 degrees declination aligned to a significant gap down in price. More recently at the end of July 2023, Lean hogs price recorded an interim high just as Mars was at 0 degrees declination and Moon was at maximum declination.

For 2024:

- ☼ **Mars will pass through 1-degree of declination during the time around June 22**

- ☼ **Venus will pass 2-degrees declination around February 23, June 23, and October 6.**

- ☼ **Moon will be at its declination maximum January 23, February 19, March 18, April 13, May 11, June 7, July 5, August 1, August 28, September 24, October 21, November 18, and December 16.**

CHAPTER EIGHT

Quantum Science

Quantum Lines Math

Quantum Price Lines are based on Einstein's quantum theory. The notion of Quantum Lines posits that the price of a stock, index or commodity can be thought of as a light particle or electron that can occupy different energy levels or orbital shells.

Author and market researcher Fabio Oreste combined the notion of quantum price lines with Einstein's theory that the planets can cause the fabric of space-time to be bent. Picture a group of people holding the edges of a large blanket. They pull on the edges until the blanket is stretched tight. Next, someone places a ball on the tight blanket. The weight of the ball causes a slight sag in the blanket fabric. Next the ball is moved to a different location on the blanket, where the weight of the ball once again causes a sag. The two points of sag are then joined by a line that is sketched onto the blanket. Oreste says the line joining these two points where the ball has caused the blanket to sag is akin to a

Quantum Price Line. In his book entitled *Quantum Trading,* [1] Oreste details his formula for Quantum Price Line calculation:

Quantum Line = (N x 360) + PSO ;

Where N is the harmonic level = 1,2,3,4,5,6,8,…

Always think of harmonics in terms of even whole number divisions of a circle. A 3rd harmonic (N=3) is 120-degrees. A 5th harmonic (N=5) is 360/5 =72 degrees. And so on.

Where PSO = heliocentric planetary longitude x Conversion Scale

The Conversion Scale = 2^n ; 1,2,4,8,16,…; where n=0,1,2,3,4,….

When dealing with prices less than 360, the inverse variation of the formula is used.

Quantum Line = (1/N x 360) + PSO

Oreste's technique then allows one to calculate various sub-divisions of these Quantum Lines. For example, if one calculated a 3rd harmonic and a 4th harmonic quantum line, one could then calculate the ¼, ½, and ¾ sub-divisions of the distance between the lines.

Please note the use of *heliocentric* planetary data in these Quantum Line calculations. There are websites that will provide you with this data such as **www.astro.com/swisseph**. Appendix B at the back of this book contains some heliocentric data for the outer planets. Alternatively, you can purchase a Heliocentric Ephemeris book such as *The American Heliocentric Ephemeris, 2001-2050.*

To assist you with calculating Quantum Lines, consider the following example:

On a given date, suppose the following heliocentric planetary positions are noted: Mars 306 degrees, Jupiter 307 degrees, Neptune 324 degrees, Pluto 271 degrees.

In this example, let N=1 and let the conversion scale be set to CS=1. PSO will be the planetary longitude x CS.

The Oreste point of maximum curvature for these planets is then:

Mars: (N x 360) + PSO; which is (1 x360) + 306 = 666
Jupiter: 360 + 307 = 667
Neptune: 360 + 324 = 684
Pluto: 360 + 271 = 631

If you were to take another date in the future and calculate the points of maximum curvature, you could then join the two points for each planet. By definition two points joined equals a straight line. You could then extend these lines out into the future. These lines are the *Quantum Lines* (or QLs).

If the above maximum curvature numbers seem oddly familiar, think to early 2009 and consider: The S&P 500 at the March 6, 2009 low delivered an intra-day price of 665.7 and the close for the day was 687. Indeed, Mars, Jupiter and Neptune all acted in concert on March 6, 2009 to provide a floor of support under the US equity market.

For larger price values such as those in an equity index, it becomes necessary to use a bigger value for N. Consider the following more recent example of the S&P 500. The high on the S&P 500 on September 7, 2021 was 4546. Intuitively, a larger number such as this will demand something more than N=1 and CS=1. The question is, are there Oreste points of maximum curvature at or near this level that would suggest the S&P 500 had hit a significant resistance level?

The first step in answering this question is to obtain the heliocentric planetary data for the date in question. Positions of planets were:

Mars at 180-degrees, Jupiter at 328, Neptune at 351, Saturn at 311, and Pluto at 295-degrees.

Next, choose a CS value. Given the magnitude of the S&P 500, consider using CS=23 = 8.

The Quantum Line formula is:

(N x 360) + (heliocentric position x conversion scale)

Calculating the back half of the formula gives us:

> Mars: 8x180 = 1440
> Jupiter: 8x328 = 2624
> Neptune: 8x351 = 2808
> Saturn: 8x311 = 2488
> Pluto: 8x295 = 2360

Next, a harmonic N value is required. Consider the 5th harmonic of N=5.

The formula then yields:

> Mars: (5x360) + 1440 = 3240
> Jupiter: (5x360) + 2624 = 4424
> Neptune: (5x360) + 2808 = 4608

Saturn: (5x360) +2488 = 4288
Pluto: (5x360) + 2360 = 4160

From these numbers we can conclude that a Neptune 5th harmonic at 4608 was foretelling of overhead resistance on September 7, 2021.

Next, consider the 6th harmonic and N=6x360 = 2160.

The recalculated values become:

Mars: (6x360) + 1440 = 3600
Jupiter: (6x360) + 2624 = 4784
Neptune: (6x360) + 2808 = 4968
Saturn: (6x360) + 2488 = 4648
Pluto: (6x360) + 2360 = 4520

From these numbers we can conclude that the Pluto 6th harmonic at 4520 was playing a key role in the price action of the S&P 500. A Saturn 6th harmonic was situated close by. In the weeks that followed, the S&P 500 dropped over 200 points.

Calculating Quantum Lines is onerous initially. However, with practice the task becomes easier. What follows is a suggested list of some points of maximum curvature you can apply to various indices and commodities for 2024.

These various points are based on the following heliocentric planetary positions at January 1, July 1, and December 30, 2024. As 2024 begins, sketch the Jan 1 and July 1 points on your charts. Join the points with a line. Later in 2024, add the December 30 point and extend your lines.

HELIOCENTRIC DEGREE POSITION			
Planet	Jan 1, 2024	July 1, 2024	Dec 30, 2024
Jupiter	45	62	78
Saturn	337	343	349
Neptune	356	358	359
Uranus	51	53	55
Pluto	299	300	301

2024 Quantum Levels

S&P 500 Index (CS=64)

PLANET & HARMONIC	JAN 1	JULY 1	DEC 30
Jupiter 1st	3240	4328	5352
Jupiter 2nd	3600	4688	-
Jupiter 3rd	3960	5048	-
Jupiter 4th	4320	5408	-
Jupiter 5th	4680	5768	-
Jupiter 6th	5040	-	-

S&P 500 Index (CS=64)

PLANET & HARMONIC	JAN 1	JULY 1	DEC 30
Uranus 1st	3624	3752	3880
Uranus 2nd	3984	4112	4240
Uranus 3rd	4344	4472	4600
Uranus 4th	4704	4832	4960
Uranus 5th	5064	5192	5320
Uranus 6th	-	-	-

S&P 500 Index (CS=8)

PLANET & HARMONIC	JAN 1	JULY 1	DEC 30
Saturn 2nd	3416	3464	3512
Saturn 3rd	3776	3824	3872
Saturn 4th	4136	4184	4232
Saturn 5th	4496	4544	4592
Saturn 6th	4856	4904	4952
Saturn 8th	5576	5624	5672
Neptune 2nd	3568	3584	3592
Neptune 3rd	3928	3944	3952
Neptune 4th	4288	4304	4312
Neptune 5th	4648	4664	4672
Neptune 6th	5008	5024	5032
Neptune 8th	5728	5744	5752
Pluto 2nd	3112	3120	3128
Pluto 3rd	3472	3480	3488
Pluto 4th	3832	3840	3848
Pluto 5th	4192	4200	4208
Pluto 6th	4552	4560	4568
Pluto 8th	5272	5280	5288

NASDAQ Composite Index (CS=32)

PLANET & HARMONIC	JAN 1	JULY 1	DEC 30
Saturn 12th	15104	15296	15488
Saturn 15th	16184	16376	16568
Saturn 16th	16544	16736	16928
Saturn 18th	17264	17456	17648
Saturn 20th	17984	18176	18368
Neptune 12th	15712	15776	15808
Neptune 15th	16792	16856	16888
Neptune 16th	17152	17216	17248
Neptune 18th	17872	17936	17968

Neptune 20th	18592	18656	18688
Pluto 12th	13888	13920	13952
Pluto 15th	14968	15000	15032
Pluto 16th	15328	15360	15392
Pluto 18th	16048	16080	16112
Pluto 20th	16768	16800	16832

NASDAQ Composite Index (CS=32)

PLANET & HARMONIC	JAN 1	JULY 1	DEC 30
Neptune 8th	14272	14336	14368
Neptune 9th	14632	14696	14728
Neptune 10th	14992	15056	15088
Neptune 12th	15712	15776	15808
Neptune 15th	16792	16856	16888
Neptune 16th	17152	17216	17248
Neptune 18th	17872	17936	17968
Neptune 20th	18592	18656	18688

NASDAQ Composite Index (CS=256)

PLANET & HARMONIC	JAN 1	JULY 1	DEC 30
Jupiter 1st	11880	16232	20328
Jupiter 2nd	12240	16592	20688
Jupiter 3rd	12600	16952	21048
Jupiter 4th	12960	17312	21408
Jupiter 5th	13320	17672	21768
Jupiter 6th	13680	18032	-
Jupiter 8th	14400	18752	-
Jupiter 9th	14760	19112	-
Jupiter 10th	15120	19472	-
Jupiter 12th	14840	20192	-
Jupiter 15th	16920	21272	-
Jupiter 16th	17280	-	-
Jupiter 18th	18000	-	-

S&P ASX 200 Index (CS=16)

PLANET & HARMONIC	JAN 1	JULY 1	DEC 30
Saturn 4th	6832	6928	7024
Saturn 5th	7192	7288	7384
Saturn 6th	7552	7648	7744
Saturn 8th	8272	8368	8464
Saturn 9th	8632	8728	8824
Saturn 10th	8992	9088	9184
Saturn 8th	8096	8192	8240

S&P ASX 200 Index (CS=16)

PLANET & HARMONIC	JAN 1	JULY 1	DEC 30
Neptune 1st	6056	6088	6104
Neptune 2nd	6416	6448	6464
Neptune 3rd	6776	6808	6824
Neptune 4th	7136	7168	7184
Neptune 5th	7496	7528	7544
Neptune 6th	7856	7888	7904
Neptune 8th	8576	8608	8624
Neptune 9th	8936	8968	8984
Neptune 10th	9296	9328	9344

S&P ASX 200 Index (CS=16)

PLANET & HARMONIC	JAN 1	JULY 1	DEC 30
Pluto 5th	6584	6600	6616
Pluto 6th	6944	6960	6976
Pluto 8th	7664	7680	7696
Pluto 9th	8024	8040	8056
Pluto 10th	8384	8400	8416
Pluto 12th	9104	9120	9136

Gold Futures (CS=2)

PLANET & HARMONIC	JAN 1	JULY 1	DEC 30
Saturn 3rd	1754	1766	1778
Saturn 4th	2114	2126	2138
Saturn 5th	2474	2486	2498
Neptune 3rd	1792	1796	1798
Neptune 4th	2152	2156	2158
Neptune 5th	2512	2516	2518
Pluto 3rd	1678	1680	1682
Pluto 4th	2038	2040	2042
Pluto 4th	2398	2400	2402

Gold Futures (CS=2)

PLANET & HARMONIC	JAN 1	JULY 1	DEC 30
Jupiter 1st	1800	2344	2856
Jupiter 2nd	2160	2704	3216
Jupiter 3rd	2520	-	-
Jupiter 4th	2880	-	-

Silver Futures (CS=1/64)

PLANET & HARMONIC	JAN 1	JULY 1	DEC 30
Jupiter 12th	$30.72	$30.96	$31.21
Jupiter 16th	$23.20	$23.48	$23.71
Jupiter 18th	$20.70	$20.99	$21.21
Jupiter 20th	$18.70	$19.01	$19.21
Saturn 12th	$35.25	$35.35	$35.44
Saturn 16th	$27.75	$27.85	$27.94
Saturn 18th	$25.25	$25.35	$25.44
Saturn 20th	$23.25	$23.35	$23.44
Neptune 12th	$35.55	$35.58	$35.60

Neptune 16th	$28.05	$28.08	$28.10
Neptune 18th	$25.55	$25.58	$25.60
Neptune 20th	$23.55	$23.58	$23.60
Pluto 12th	$34.66	$34.68	$34.69
Pluto 16th	$27.16	$27.18	$27.19
Pluto 18th	$24.66	$24.68	$24.69
Pluto 20th	$22.66	$22.68	$22.69

Currency Futures (Canadian dollar, Australian dollar) CS=1/1024

PLANET & HARMONIC	JAN 1	JULY 1	DEC 30
Saturn 4th	$0.9032	$0.9033	$0.9034
Saturn 5th	$0.7232	$0.7233	$0.7234
Saturn 6th	$0.6032	$0.6033	$0.6034
Neptune 4th	$0.9034	$0.9034	$0.9035
Neptune 5th	$0.7234	$0.7234	$0.7235
Neptune 6th	$0.6034	$0.6034	$0.6035
Pluto 4th	$0.9029	$0.9029	$0.9029
Pluto 5th	$0.7229	$0.7229	$0.7229
Pluto 6th	$0.6029	$0.6029	$0.6029

Currency Futures (Euro and British pound) CS=1/256

PLANET & HARMONIC	JAN 1	JULY 1	DEC 30
Jupiter 3rd	$1.2001	$1.2024	$1.2030
Jupiter 4th	$0.9001	$0.9024	$0.9030
Saturn 3rd	$1.2065	$1.2066	$1.2068
Saturn 4th	$0.9065	$1.9065	$1.9068
Neptune 3rd	$1.2138	$1.2139	$1.2140
Neptune 4th	$0.91388	$0.91396	$0.9140
Pluto 3rd	$1.2058	$1.2058	$1.2058
Pluto 4th	$0.9058	$0.9058	$0.9058

Wheat and Corn Futures CS=1/64

PLANET & HARMONIC	JAN 1	JULY 1	DEC 30
Saturn 2nd	$18.526	$18.535	$18.545
Saturn 3rd	$12.526	$12.536	$12.545
Saturn 4th	$9.526	$9.953	$9.545
Saturn 5th	$7.772	$7.776	$7.745
Saturn 6th	$6.526	$6.535	$6.545
Neptune 2nd	$18.556	$18.559	$18.560
Neptune 3rd	$12.556	$12.559	$12.560
Neptune 4th	$9.556	$9.559	$9.560
Neptune 5th	$7.756	$7.759	$7.760
Neptune 6th	$6.556	$6.559	$6.560

Wheat and Corn Futures CS=1/32

PLANET & HARMONIC	JAN 1	JULY 1	DEC 30
Saturn 3rd	$13.053	$13.071	$13.090
Saturn 4th	$10.053	$10.071	$10.090
Saturn 5th	$8.253	$8.271	$8.290
Saturn 6th	$7.053	$7.071	$7.090
Saturn 8th	$5.553	$5.571	$5.590
Neptune 3rd	$13.112	$13.112	$13.121
Neptune 4th	$10.112	$10.118	$10.121
Neptune 5th	$8.312	$8.318	$8.321
Neptune 6th	$7.112	$7.118	$7.121
Neptune 8th	$5.612	$5.618	$5.621

Wheat and Corn Futures CS=1/32

PLANET & HARMONIC	JAN 1	JULY 1	DEC 30
Pluto 3rd	$12.934	$12.937	$12.940
Pluto 4th	$9.934	$9.937	$9.940
Pluto 5th	$8.134	$8.137	$8.140
Pluto 6th	$6.934	$6.937	$6.940
Pluto 8th	$5.434	$5.437	$5.440

Soybean Futures CS=3

PLANET & HARMONIC	JAN 1	JULY 1	DEC 30
Saturn 1st	$13.71	$13.89	$14.07
Saturn 2nd	$17.31	$17.49	$17.67
Saturn 3rd	$20.91	$21.09	$21.27
Neptune 1st	$14.28	$14.34	$17.97
Neptune 2nd	$17.88	$21.54	$21.57
Neptune 3rd	$21.48	$11.85	$11.88

WTI Crude Oil Futures CS=1/4

PLANET & HARMONIC	JAN 1	JULY 1	DEC 30
Saturn 6th	$102.12	$102.87	$103.62
Saturn 8th	$87.12	$87.87	$88.62
Saturn 9th	$82.12	$82.87	$83.62
Saturn 10th	$78.12	$78.87	$79.62
Saturn 12th	$72.12	$72.87	$73.62
Saturn 16th	$64.62	$65.37	$66.12
Neptune 8th	$89.5	$89.75	$89.87
Neptune 9th	$84.5	$84.75	$84.87
Neptune 10th	$80.5	$80.75	$80.87
Neptune 12th	$74.5	$74.75	$74.87
Neptune 16th	$67	$67.25	$67.37
Neptune 18th	$64.5	$64.75	$64.87

FINAL WORDS

I have taken you on a wide-ranging journey in this book to acquaint you with the mathematical links between planetary activity and market price behavior. I sincerely hope you will embrace planetary cycles as a valuable tool to assist you in your trading and investing activity. I hope you will pause often to contemplate whether the correlations you have learned about in this book are the actions of the cosmos on the emotions of traders and investors or the actions of power players using the planets to manipulate the markets.

If you decide to embrace financial astrology as a tool to help you navigate the markets, I encourage you to stick with it. At first it might seem daunting, but fight the urge to give up. Soon enough, your trading and investing activity will take on a new meaning.

To encourage you, I will leave you with the words of Neil Turok from his 2012 book, *The Universe Within:* [1]

"Perseverance leads to enlightenment. And the truth is more beautiful than your wildest dreams."

NOTES

&

RECOMMENDED

READING

Introduction

1) McWhirter, L. (1938) *McWhirter Theory of Stock Market Forecasting.* Astro Book Company, USA.
2) Bradley, D. (1948) *Stock Market Prediction.* Llewellyn Publishers, USA.

Chapter 1

Figure 1-1: taken from Loes Ten Kate, I. (2006) *Organics on Mars -Laboratory studies of organic material under simulated Martian conditions.* Ph.D. Thesis.

Figure 1-2: taken from **www.wikimediacommons.com**. File Earths orbit and ecliptic.PNG

Figure 1-3: taken from **https://www.elsaelsa.com/astrology/ zodiac-sign-glyphs**

Figure 1-4: taken from **http://mysticaltransformations.com**

Figure 1-5: taken from **https://serc.carleton.edu/mel/teaching_resources/moon_mel.html**

Figure 1-8: taken from **http://www.astronomy.ohio-state.edu/~pogge/Ast161/Unit2**

Chapter 3

1) McWhirter, L. (1938) *McWhirter Theory of Stock Market Forecasting.* Astro Book Company, USA.

Chapter 4

1) Cahn, J. (2011) *The Harbinger.* Charisma Media, USA.
2) Cahn, J. (2016) *The Book of Mysteries.* Charisma Media, USA.
3) Cahn, J. (2017) *The Paradigm.* Charisma Media, USA.
4) Wong, M.(2005) Tunnel Through the Air. *Traders World.* Issue 39, p.46.

Chapter 5

1) Seddon,C. (2021) *Mercury: Elusive Messenger of the Gods.* Glanville Press, USA
2) Long, J. (1992) *Basic astrotech: A new technique for trading commodities using geocosmic energy fields with technical analysis.* 6th ed. Professional Astrology Service Inc. USA.
3) Bradley, D. (2004) *Stock Market Prediction: The Historical and Future Siderograph Charts.* Books Work. USA.
4) Kramer, J. (1995) *Astrology Really Works.* Hay House, USA.
5) Gann, W.D. (1927) *Tunnel Through the Air.* Pantainos Classics, USA.

Chapter 6

1) McWhirter, L. (1938) *McWhirter Theory of Stock Market Forecasting*. Astro Book Company, USA.

Chapter 8

1) Oreste, F. (2011) *Quantum Trading*. J. Wiley & Sons, USA.

Final Words

1) Turok, N. (2012) *The Universe Within*. House of Anansi Press, Canada.

Follow the Trend, M.G, Bucholtz, (Canada 2023).

The Cosmic Clock, M.G. Bucholtz (Canada, 2016).

Stock Market Forecasting – The McWhirter Method De-Mystified, M.G. Bucholtz, (Canada, 2014).

A Theory of Continuous Planet Interaction, *NCGR Research Journal*, T. Waterfall, Volume 4, Spring 2014, pp 67-87.

The Bull, the Bear and the Planets, M.G. Bucholtz, (USA, 2013).

The Lost Science, M.G. Bucholtz, (USA, 2013)

Financial Astrology, Giacomo Albano, (UK, 2011)

The Universal Clock, J. Long, (USA, 1995)

GLOSSARY

Ascendant: one of four cardinal points on a horoscope, the Ascendant denotes the constellation visible at a given time on the eastern horizon

Aspect: the angular relationship between two planets measured in degrees

Autumnal Equinox (see Equinox): – the time of year when Sun is at 0-degrees Libra

Conjunct: an angular relationship of 0-degrees between two planets

Cosmo-biology: changes in human emotion caused by changes in cosmic energy

Declination: the amount (in degrees) that a planet wanders above or below the ecliptic plane as measured using heliocentric data

Descendant: one of four cardinal points on a horoscope, the Descendant denotes the constellation visible at a given time on the western horizon

Ecliptic Plane: the plane of motion traveled by the planets as they orbit the Sun

Elongation: the angle subtended between a planet and the Sun based on an observer's position on Earth

Ephemeris: a daily tabular compilation of planetary and lunar positions

Equinox: an event occurring twice annually that marks the time when the tilt of the Earth's axis is neither toward nor away from the Sun

Fibonacci Sequence: a recursive mathematical sequence in which a given term is the sum of the two preceding terms. (The infinite sequence is as follows: 0,1,1,2,3,5,8,13,21,34,55,89…)

First Trade chart: a zodiac chart depicting the positions of the planets at the time a company's stock or a commodity future commenced trading on a recognized financial exchange

First Trade date: the date a stock or commodity futures contract first began trading on a recognized exchange

Full Moon: from a vantage point situated on Earth, when the Moon is seen to be 180-degrees to the Sun

Gann Master Cycle: the 19.86-year time span from heliocentric Saturn and Jupiter being conjunct to once again being conjunct

Geocentric: planetary location system in which the vantage point for determining planetary aspects is the Earth

Heliocentric: planetary location system in which the vantage point for determining planetary aspects is the Sun

Horoscope: an image of the zodiac overlaid with the positions of the planets

House: a 1/12th portion of the zodiac. Portions are not necessarily equal depending on the mathematical formula used to calculate the divisions

Lunar Month: (see Synodic Month)

Lunation: (see New Moon)

McWhirter Cycle: The 18.6-year time span in which the North Node progresses around the 12 zodiac signs

Mid-Heaven: one of four cardinal points on a horoscope, situated in the South

Natal: the position of a planet at the time of creation of a futures contract, or the IPO of a stock

New Moon: when the Moon is seen to be 0-degrees to the Sun.

North Node of Moon: the intersection points between the Moon's plane and Earth's ecliptic are termed the North and South nodes (Astrologers tend to focus on the North node and Ephemeris tables list the zodiacal position of the North Node for each calendar day.)

Orb: the amount of flexibility or tolerance given to an aspect

Quantum Point: a mathematical construct that refers to the point of maximum distortion of the time-space fabric due to the presence of a planet

Retrograde motion: the apparent backwards motion of a planet through the zodiac signs when viewed from a vantage point on Earth

Sidereal Month: the Moon orbits Earth with a slightly elliptical pattern in approximately 27.3 days, relative to a fixed frame of reference

Sidereal Orbital Period: the time required for a planet to make one full orbit of the Sun as viewed from a fixed vantage point on the Sun.

Siderograph: a mathematical equation developed by astrologer Donald Bradley in 1946. (By plotting the output of the equation against the date, inflection points can be seen on the plotted curve. It is at these inflection points that human emotion is most apt to change resulting in a trend change on the Dow Jones or S&P 500 Index.)

Solstice: occurring twice annually, a solstice event marks the time when the Sun reaches its highest or lowest altitude above the horizon at noon

Synodic Month: from a moving frame of reference, the 29.5-day time span for the Moon to orbit the Earth

Synodic Orbital Period: the time required for a planet to make one full orbit of the Sun as viewed from a fixed vantage point on Earth

Transiting: the action of a planet moving past a selected point of the zodiac wheel

Vernal Equinox: the time of the year when Sun is at 0-degrees Aries

Zodiac: an imaginary band encircling the 360-degrees of the planetary system divided into twelve equal portions of 30-degrees each

Zodiac Wheel: a circular image broken into 12 portions of 30-degrees each. Each portion represents a different astrological sign

ABOUT THE AUTHOR

Malcolm Bucholtz, B.Sc, MBA, M.Sc., is a graduate of Queen's University (Faculty of Engineering) in Canada and Heriot Watt University in Scotland (where he received an MBA degree and a M.Sc. degree). After working in Canadian industry for far too many years, Malcolm followed his passion for the financial markets by becoming an Investment Advisor/Commodity Trading Advisor with an independent brokerage firm in western Canada. Today, he resides in Saskatchewan, Canada where he trades the financial markets using technical chart analysis, esoteric mathematics, and the planetary principles outlined in this book.

Malcolm is the author of several books. His first book, *The Bull, the Bear and the Planets,* offers the reader an introduction to financial astrology and makes the case that there are esoteric and astrological phenomena that influence the financial markets. His second book, *The Lost Science,* takes the reader on a deeper journey into planetary events and unique mathematical phenomena that influence financial markets. His third book, *De-Mystifying the McWhirter Theory of Stock Market Forecasting* seeks to simplify and illustrate the McWhirter methodology. *The Cosmic Clock* follows from the *Lost Science* and helps the reader become better acquainted with planetary events that influence markets. Malcolm has been writing the *Financial Astrology Almanac* each year since 2014. In 2023 he also released *Follow the Trend*, a book to assist traders and investors in identifying price trend changes on indices, stocks, and commodity futures.

Malcolm maintains a website (www.investingsuccess.ca) where he provides traders and investors with astrological insights into the financial markets. He also offers the *Astrology Letter* service where subscribers receive twice-monthly previews of pending astrological events that stand to influence markets. He also offers the *Cycle Report* where subscribers are kept apprised on cyclical turning points based on Hurst cycles.

OTHER BOOKS BY THE AUTHOR

Follow The Trend

Geopolitical unrest, interest rates, inflation, financial blogs, financial media channels all touting the latest, greatest investment ideas, fund managers with rock star-like status. The emotions of traders and investors are continually being pulled in multiple directions at once. At times the noise can be deafening. What to buy? When to buy? When to sell?

This book introduces the reader to the concept of the *trend*. Is price moving in a bullish direction or bearish direction? How does one know when the trend is changing? Paying attention to changes of trend on a stock, an index, an ETF, or a commodity futures contract can help traders and investors tune out the noise and re-gain a sense of clarity.

The trend is seldom mentioned in financial media. Instead, the media serves up a constant stream of angst and drama. Financial advisors seldom pay attention to the trend, preferring instead to promote the idea of buying and holding.

This book pushes back against this status quo. There was a time when the trend *was* followed. In the 1930s, H.M. Gartley introduced the use of major and intermediate trend lines on a price chart. W.D. Gann used swing points on price charts to gain insight into the trend. The 1980s and 1990s heralded computer algorithms and chart technical indicators to help delineate changes in trend.

This book shows the reader how to apply trend lines and swing points to making buy and sell decisions. This book goes on to examine a number of chart technical indicators. How are they mathematically structured? What do they reveal about the trend? How should they be interpreted? Are some better than others? This book provides insight into the mathematical structure of the various types of indicators. These questions are all answered for the reader.

This book will change the way the reader looks at the financial markets. This book will help the reader tune out the noise. This book will give the reader the skills and ability to answer the two critical questions: when to buy? And when to sell?

The Cosmic Clock

THE COSMIC CLOCK
TIMING THE FINANCIAL
MARKETS USING
THE PLANETS
M.G. Bucholtz, B.Sc, MBA

Can the movements of the Moon affect the stock market?

Are price swings on Crude Oil, Soybeans, the British pound and other financial instruments a reflection of planetary placements?

The answer to these questions is YES. Changes in price trends on the markets are in fact related to our changing emotions. Our emotions, in turn, are impacted by the changing events in our cosmos.

In the early part of the 20th century, many successful traders on Wall Street, including the venerable W.D. Gann and the mysterious Louise McWhirter, understood that emotion was linked to the forces of the cosmos. They used astrological events and esoteric mathematics to predict changes in price trend and to profit from the markets.

However, by the latter part of the 20th century, the investment community had become more comfortable in relying on academic financial theory and the opinions of colorful television media personalities, all wrapped up in a buy and hold mentality.

The Cosmic Clock has been written for traders and investors who are seeking to gain an understanding of the cosmic forces that influence emotion and the financial markets.

This book will acquaint you with an extensive range of astrological and mathematical phenomena. From the Golden Mean and Fibonacci Sequence through planetary transit lines, quantum lines, the McWhirter method, planetary conjunctions and market cycles. The numerous illustrated examples show how these unique phenomena can deepen your understanding of the financial markets with the goal of making you a better trader and investor.

Stock Market Forecasting -
The McWhirter Method
De-Mystified

M.G. Bucholtz, B.Sc., MBA

Stock Market Forecasting: The McWhirter Method De-Mystified

Very little is known about Louise McWhirter, except that in 1937 she wrote the book, *McWhirter Theory of Stock Market Forecasting*.

In my travels to places as far away as the British Library in London, England to research financial Astrology, not once did I come across any other books by her. Not once did I find any other book from her era that even mentioned her name. I find all of this to be deeply mysterious. Whoever she was, she wrote only one book. It is a powerful one that is as accurate today as it was back in 1937. The purpose of writing this book is suggested by the title itself – to de-mystify McWhirter's methodology.

The Lost Science

The financial markets are a reflection of the psychological emotions of traders and investors. These emotions ebb and flow in harmony with the forces of nature.

Scientific techniques and phenomena such as square root mathematics, the Golden Mean, the Golden Sequence, lunar events, planetary transits and planetary aspects have been used by civilizations dating as far back as the ancient Egyptians in order to comprehend the forces of nature.

The emotions of traders and investors can fluctuate in accordance with these forces of nature. Lunar events can be seen to align with trend changes on financial markets. Significant market cycles align with planetary transits and aspects. Price patterns on stocks, commodity futures and market indices can be seen to conform to square root and Golden Mean mathematics.

In the early years of the 20th century the most successful traders on Wall Street, including the venerable W.D. Gann, used these scientific techniques and phenomena to profit from the markets. However, over the ensuing decades as technology has advanced, the science has been lost.

The Lost Science acquaints the reader with an extensive range of astrological and mathematical phenomena. From the Golden Mean and Fibonacci Sequence, to planetary transit lines and square roots through to an examination of lunar and planetary aspects, the numerous illustrated examples in this book show the reader how these unique scientific phenomena impact the financial markets.

The Bull, The Bear and The Planets

Once maligned by many, the subject of financial astrology is now experiencing a revival as traders and investors seek deeper insight into the forces that move the financial markets.

The markets are a dynamic entity fueled by many factors, some of which we can easily comprehend, some of which are esoteric. *The Bull, The Bear and the Planets* introduces the reader to the notion that astrological

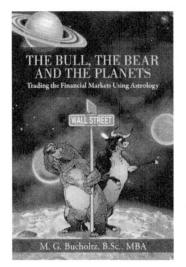

phenomena can influence price action on financial markets and create trend changes across both short and longer term time horizons. From an introduction to the historical basics behind astrology through to an examination of lunar astrology and planetary aspects, the numerous illustrated examples in this book will introduce the reader to the power of astrology and its impact on both equity markets and commodity futures markets.

APPENDIX A
Geocentric Data

	Moon	Sun	Mercury	Venus	Mars
Jan 1 2024	158.46	280.25	262.25	242.87	267.46
Jan 2 2024	170.27	281.27	262.18	244.08	268.2
Jan 3 2024	182.08	282.29	262.27	245.3	268.95
Jan 4 2024	193.99	283.31	262.49	246.52	269.69
Jan 5 2024	206.09	284.33	262.85	247.74	270.44
Jan 6 2024	218.46	285.35	263.32	248.96	271.18
Jan 7 2024	231.2	286.37	263.9	250.18	271.93
Jan 8 2024	244.36	287.39	264.57	251.4	272.67
Jan 9 2024	257.98	288.41	265.33	252.62	273.42
Jan 10 2024	272.05	289.43	266.16	253.85	274.17
Jan 11 2024	286.5	290.44	267.06	255.07	274.92
Jan 12 2024	301.22	291.46	268.02	256.3	275.67
Jan 13 2024	316.09	292.48	269.04	257.52	276.42
Jan 14 2024	330.94	293.5	270.1	258.75	277.17
Jan 15 2024	345.65	294.52	271.2	259.97	277.92
Jan 16 2024	0.12	295.54	272.35	261.2	278.67
Jan 17 2024	14.3	296.56	273.53	262.43	279.42
Jan 18 2024	28.17	297.58	274.74	263.66	280.18
Jan 19 2024	41.76	298.6	275.98	264.89	280.93
Jan 20 2024	55.09	299.61	277.25	266.11	281.68
Jan 21 2024	68.18	300.63	278.54	267.34	282.44
Jan 22 2024	81.07	301.65	279.85	268.57	283.19
Jan 23 2024	93.77	302.67	281.19	269.8	283.95
Jan 24 2024	106.3	303.68	282.54	271.03	284.71
Jan 25 2024	118.67	304.7	283.91	272.27	285.46
Jan 26 2024	130.87	305.72	285.3	273.5	286.22
Jan 27 2024	142.93	306.73	286.71	274.73	286.98
Jan 28 2024	154.87	307.75	288.13	275.96	287.74
Jan 29 2024	166.7	308.76	289.56	277.19	288.5
Jan 30 2024	178.49	309.78	291.01	278.43	289.26
Jan 31 2024	190.3	310.79	292.48	279.66	290.02

	Moon	Sun	Mercury	Venus	Mars
Feb 1 2024	202.18	311.81	293.95	280.89	290.78
Feb 2 2024	214.24	312.82	295.44	282.13	291.55
Feb 3 2024	226.55	313.84	296.95	283.36	292.31
Feb 4 2024	239.22	314.85	298.46	284.6	293.07
Feb 5 2024	252.3	315.87	299.99	285.83	293.84
Feb 6 2024	265.87	316.88	301.53	287.07	294.6
Feb 7 2024	279.93	317.9	303.09	288.3	295.36
Feb 8 2024	294.46	318.91	304.65	289.54	296.13
Feb 9 2024	309.36	319.92	306.23	290.77	296.9
Feb 10 2024	324.49	320.94	307.83	292.01	297.66
Feb 11 2024	339.68	321.95	309.43	293.25	298.43
Feb 12 2024	354.76	322.96	311.05	294.48	299.2
Feb 13 2024	9.59	323.97	312.69	295.72	299.97
Feb 14 2024	24.06	324.98	314.33	296.96	300.73
Feb 15 2024	38.15	325.99	315.99	298.19	301.5
Feb 16 2024	51.83	327	317.67	299.43	302.27
Feb 17 2024	65.14	328.01	319.36	300.67	303.04
Feb 18 2024	78.13	329.02	321.06	301.9	303.81
Feb 19 2024	90.83	330.03	322.78	303.14	304.58
Feb 20 2024	103.31	331.04	324.52	304.38	305.35
Feb 21 2024	115.6	332.05	326.27	305.61	306.12
Feb 22 2024	127.74	333.06	328.03	306.85	306.89
Feb 23 2024	139.75	334.06	329.82	308.09	307.67
Feb 24 2024	151.67	335.07	331.61	309.33	308.44
Feb 25 2024	163.52	336.08	333.43	310.56	309.21
Feb 26 2024	175.34	337.08	335.25	311.8	309.98
Feb 27 2024	187.14	338.09	337.1	313.04	310.76
Feb 28 2024	198.99	339.09	338.96	314.28	311.53
Feb 29 2024	210.93	340.09	340.83	315.51	312.3

	Moon	Sun	Mercury	Venus	Mars
Mar 1 2024	223.02	341.1	342.72	316.75	313.08
Mar 2 2024	235.34	342.1	344.62	317.99	313.85
Mar 3 2024	247.96	343.1	346.53	319.23	314.63
Mar 4 2024	260.96	344.11	348.46	320.46	315.4
Mar 5 2024	274.39	345.11	350.39	321.7	316.18
Mar 6 2024	288.28	346.11	352.33	322.94	316.95
Mar 7 2024	302.64	347.11	354.27	324.18	317.73
Mar 8 2024	317.42	348.11	356.21	325.42	318.51
Mar 9 2024	332.5	349.11	358.15	326.66	319.28
Mar 10 2024	347.73	350.11	0.08	327.89	320.06
Mar 11 2024	2.96	351.11	1.99	329.13	320.84
Mar 12 2024	18.01	352.11	3.89	330.37	321.61
Mar 13 2024	32.76	353.11	5.76	331.61	322.39
Mar 14 2024	47.1	354.11	7.61	332.85	323.17
Mar 15 2024	60.99	355.1	9.41	334.08	323.95
Mar 16 2024	74.45	356.1	11.16	335.32	324.72
Mar 17 2024	87.5	357.1	12.86	336.56	325.5
Mar 18 2024	100.2	358.09	14.5	337.8	326.28
Mar 19 2024	112.6	359.08	16.07	339.03	327.06
Mar 20 2024	124.77	0.08	17.56	340.27	327.84
Mar 21 2024	136.78	1.07	18.96	341.51	328.61
Mar 22 2024	148.67	2.06	20.27	342.74	329.39
Mar 23 2024	160.5	3.06	21.48	343.98	330.17
Mar 24 2024	172.31	4.05	22.58	345.22	330.95
Mar 25 2024	184.13	5.04	23.58	346.45	331.73
Mar 26 2024	196.01	6.03	24.46	347.69	332.5
Mar 27 2024	207.97	7.02	25.22	348.93	333.28
Mar 28 2024	220.06	8.01	25.86	350.16	334.06
Mar 29 2024	232.31	9	26.38	351.4	334.84
Mar 30 2024	244.77	9.98	26.77	352.64	335.62
Mar 31 2024	257.49	10.97	27.04	353.87	336.39

	Moon	Sun	Mercury	Venus	Mars
Apr 1 2024	270.5	11.96	27.19	355.11	337.17
Apr 2 2024	283.86	12.94	27.21	356.34	337.95
Apr 3 2024	297.6	13.93	27.12	357.58	338.73
Apr 4 2024	311.72	14.92	26.92	358.82	339.51
Apr 5 2024	326.2	15.9	26.61	0.05	340.29
Apr 6 2024	340.99	16.89	26.21	1.29	341.06
Apr 7 2024	355.98	17.87	25.71	2.52	341.84
Apr 8 2024	11.04	18.85	25.14	3.76	342.62
Apr 9 2024	26.04	19.84	24.51	4.99	343.4
Apr 10 2024	40.83	20.82	23.82	6.23	344.17
Apr 11 2024	55.29	21.8	23.1	7.46	344.95
Apr 12 2024	69.34	22.78	22.35	8.7	345.73
Apr 13 2024	82.95	23.76	21.6	9.93	346.5
Apr 14 2024	96.13	24.74	20.85	11.17	347.28
Apr 15 2024	108.9	25.72	20.12	12.4	348.06
Apr 16 2024	121.33	26.7	19.42	13.64	348.83
Apr 17 2024	133.5	27.68	18.77	14.87	349.61
Apr 18 2024	145.46	28.66	18.16	16.1	350.38
Apr 19 2024	157.31	29.63	17.63	17.34	351.16
Apr 20 2024	169.11	30.61	17.16	18.57	351.93
Apr 21 2024	180.92	31.59	16.76	19.8	352.71
Apr 22 2024	192.8	32.56	16.44	21.04	353.48
Apr 23 2024	204.79	33.54	16.21	22.27	354.26
Apr 24 2024	216.94	34.51	16.05	23.5	355.03
Apr 25 2024	229.26	35.48	15.99	24.74	355.8
Apr 26 2024	241.78	36.46	16	25.97	356.57
Apr 27 2024	254.51	37.43	16.1	27.2	357.35
Apr 28 2024	267.48	38.4	16.27	28.43	358.12
Apr 29 2024	280.68	39.37	16.53	29.67	358.89
Apr 30 2024	294.13	40.34	16.86	30.9	359.66

	Moon	Sun	Mercury	Venus	Mars
May 1 2024	307.85	41.32	17.27	32.13	0.43
May 2 2024	321.82	42.29	17.75	33.36	1.2
May 3 2024	336.04	43.26	18.3	34.59	1.97
May 4 2024	350.48	44.23	18.91	35.83	2.74
May 5 2024	5.08	45.2	19.59	37.06	3.51
May 6 2024	19.78	46.16	20.33	38.29	4.28
May 7 2024	34.46	47.13	21.12	39.52	5.05
May 8 2024	49.02	48.1	21.98	40.75	5.81
May 9 2024	63.36	49.07	22.89	41.98	6.58
May 10 2024	77.37	50.04	23.85	43.21	7.35
May 11 2024	91	51	24.86	44.44	8.11
May 12 2024	104.23	51.97	25.92	45.68	8.88
May 13 2024	117.06	52.93	27.03	46.91	9.64
May 14 2024	129.54	53.9	28.18	48.14	10.41
May 15 2024	141.73	54.86	29.38	49.37	11.17
May 16 2024	153.7	55.83	30.62	50.6	11.93
May 17 2024	165.55	56.79	31.91	51.83	12.69
May 18 2024	177.36	57.75	33.23	53.06	13.46
May 19 2024	189.2	58.72	34.6	54.29	14.22
May 20 2024	201.15	59.68	36.01	55.52	14.98
May 21 2024	213.27	60.64	37.45	56.75	15.73
May 22 2024	225.61	61.6	38.94	57.98	16.49
May 23 2024	238.2	62.56	40.46	59.21	17.25
May 24 2024	251.04	63.53	42.03	60.44	18.01
May 25 2024	264.14	64.49	43.63	61.66	18.76
May 26 2024	277.48	65.45	45.27	62.89	19.52
May 27 2024	291.02	66.41	46.96	64.12	20.27
May 28 2024	304.74	67.37	48.67	65.35	21.03
May 29 2024	318.61	68.32	50.43	66.58	21.78
May 30 2024	332.61	69.28	52.23	67.81	22.53
May 31 2024	346.71	70.24	54.06	69.04	23.29

	Moon	Sun	Mercury	Venus	Mars
Jun 1 2024	0.91	71.2	55.93	70.27	24.04
Jun 2 2024	15.17	72.16	57.84	71.5	24.79
Jun 3 2024	29.45	73.12	59.79	72.73	25.54
Jun 4 2024	43.72	74.08	61.77	73.96	26.28
Jun 5 2024	57.89	75.03	63.78	75.19	27.03
Jun 6 2024	71.89	75.99	65.83	76.41	27.78
Jun 7 2024	85.66	76.95	67.91	77.64	28.52
Jun 8 2024	99.12	77.91	70.01	78.87	29.27
Jun 9 2024	112.25	78.86	72.14	80.1	30.01
Jun 10 2024	125.03	79.82	74.3	81.33	30.76
Jun 11 2024	137.49	80.78	76.47	82.56	31.5
Jun 12 2024	149.68	81.73	78.65	83.79	32.24
Jun 13 2024	161.66	82.69	80.84	85.02	32.98
Jun 14 2024	173.51	83.64	83.04	86.25	33.72
Jun 15 2024	185.32	84.6	85.24	87.47	34.45
Jun 16 2024	197.18	85.55	87.44	88.7	35.19
Jun 17 2024	209.18	86.51	89.63	89.93	35.93
Jun 18 2024	221.4	87.46	91.8	91.16	36.66
Jun 19 2024	233.89	88.42	93.96	92.39	37.39
Jun 20 2024	246.7	89.37	96.1	93.62	38.13
Jun 21 2024	259.85	90.32	98.21	94.85	38.86
Jun 22 2024	273.32	91.28	100.3	96.07	39.59
Jun 23 2024	287.07	92.23	102.36	97.3	40.32
Jun 24 2024	301.03	93.19	104.39	98.53	41.05
Jun 25 2024	315.15	94.14	106.39	99.76	41.77
Jun 26 2024	329.34	95.09	108.36	100.99	42.5
Jun 27 2024	343.54	96.05	110.29	102.22	43.22
Jun 28 2024	357.72	97	112.19	103.45	43.95
Jun 29 2024	11.85	97.95	114.05	104.67	44.67
Jun 30 2024	25.91	98.91	115.88	105.9	45.39

	Moon	Sun	Mercury	Venus	Mars
Jul 1 2024	39.89	99.86	117.68	107.13	46.11
Jul 2 2024	53.77	100.81	119.43	108.36	46.83
Jul 3 2024	67.53	101.77	121.16	109.59	47.55
Jul 4 2024	81.13	102.72	122.84	110.82	48.27
Jul 5 2024	94.52	103.68	124.5	112.05	48.98
Jul 6 2024	107.68	104.63	126.11	113.28	49.69
Jul 7 2024	120.57	105.58	127.69	114.51	50.41
Jul 8 2024	133.19	106.54	129.24	115.73	51.12
Jul 9 2024	145.54	107.49	130.75	116.96	51.83
Jul 10 2024	157.66	108.44	132.22	118.19	52.54
Jul 11 2024	169.6	109.4	133.66	119.42	53.24
Jul 12 2024	181.42	110.35	135.06	120.65	53.95
Jul 13 2024	193.22	111.31	136.42	121.88	54.65
Jul 14 2024	205.08	112.26	137.74	123.11	55.36
Jul 15 2024	217.09	113.21	139.02	124.34	56.06
Jul 16 2024	229.34	114.17	140.26	125.56	56.76
Jul 17 2024	241.9	115.12	141.47	126.79	57.46
Jul 18 2024	254.84	116.07	142.62	128.02	58.16
Jul 19 2024	268.18	117.03	143.74	129.25	58.85
Jul 20 2024	281.91	117.98	144.81	130.48	59.55
Jul 21 2024	296.01	118.94	145.84	131.71	60.24
Jul 22 2024	310.37	119.89	146.81	132.94	60.93
Jul 23 2024	324.91	120.85	147.74	134.17	61.62
Jul 24 2024	339.5	121.8	148.61	135.39	62.31
Jul 25 2024	354.05	122.76	149.43	136.62	63
Jul 26 2024	8.48	123.71	150.19	137.85	63.68
Jul 27 2024	22.73	124.67	150.9	139.08	64.37
Jul 28 2024	36.78	125.62	151.54	140.31	65.05
Jul 29 2024	50.63	126.58	152.12	141.54	65.73
Jul 30 2024	64.26	127.53	152.63	142.76	66.41
Jul 31 2024	77.7	128.49	153.07	143.99	67.09

	Moon	Sun	Mercury	Venus	Mars
Aug 1 2024	90.92	129.45	153.43	145.22	67.76
Aug 2 2024	103.94	130.4	153.72	146.45	68.44
Aug 3 2024	116.75	131.36	153.93	147.68	69.11
Aug 4 2024	129.34	132.32	154.06	148.91	69.78
Aug 5 2024	141.72	133.28	154.1	150.13	70.45
Aug 6 2024	153.9	134.24	154.06	151.36	71.12
Aug 7 2024	165.9	135.19	153.93	152.59	71.79
Aug 8 2024	177.78	136.15	153.71	153.82	72.45
Aug 9 2024	189.57	137.11	153.4	155.05	73.11
Aug 10 2024	201.35	138.07	153	156.27	73.77
Aug 11 2024	213.19	139.03	152.51	157.5	74.43
Aug 12 2024	225.18	139.99	151.95	158.73	75.09
Aug 13 2024	237.41	140.95	151.31	159.96	75.74
Aug 14 2024	249.96	141.91	150.61	161.18	76.39
Aug 15 2024	262.9	142.87	149.85	162.41	77.04
Aug 16 2024	276.27	143.83	149.04	163.64	77.69
Aug 17 2024	290.1	144.79	148.2	164.86	78.34
Aug 18 2024	304.35	145.75	147.34	166.09	78.99
Aug 19 2024	318.97	146.71	146.49	167.32	79.63
Aug 20 2024	333.82	147.68	145.65	168.54	80.27
Aug 21 2024	348.78	148.64	144.84	169.77	80.91
Aug 22 2024	3.71	149.6	144.08	171	81.55
Aug 23 2024	18.48	150.57	143.39	172.22	82.18
Aug 24 2024	33	151.53	142.79	173.45	82.81
Aug 25 2024	47.22	152.49	142.28	174.67	83.44
Aug 26 2024	61.11	153.46	141.88	175.9	84.07
Aug 27 2024	74.68	154.42	141.6	177.12	84.7
Aug 28 2024	87.93	155.39	141.44	178.35	85.32
Aug 29 2024	100.91	156.36	141.42	179.57	85.95
Aug 30 2024	113.64	157.32	141.53	180.8	86.57
Aug 31 2024	126.15	158.29	141.78	182.02	87.18

	Moon	Sun	Mercury	Venus	Mars
Sep 1 2024	138.46	159.26	142.17	183.25	87.8
Sep 2 2024	150.6	160.23	142.7	184.47	88.41
Sep 3 2024	162.6	161.19	143.36	185.69	89.02
Sep 4 2024	174.49	162.16	144.16	186.92	89.63
Sep 5 2024	186.29	163.13	145.08	188.14	90.23
Sep 6 2024	198.07	164.1	146.12	189.37	90.83
Sep 7 2024	209.85	165.07	147.28	190.59	91.43
Sep 8 2024	221.71	166.04	148.54	191.81	92.03
Sep 9 2024	233.71	167.02	149.89	193.03	92.63
Sep 10 2024	245.92	167.99	151.34	194.26	93.22
Sep 11 2024	258.43	168.96	152.86	195.48	93.81
Sep 12 2024	271.29	169.93	154.45	196.7	94.39
Sep 13 2024	284.58	170.91	156.1	197.92	94.98
Sep 14 2024	298.32	171.88	157.8	199.14	95.56
Sep 15 2024	312.52	172.85	159.55	200.37	96.14
Sep 16 2024	327.13	173.83	161.33	201.59	96.71
Sep 17 2024	342.07	174.8	163.13	202.81	97.28
Sep 18 2024	357.22	175.78	164.96	204.03	97.85
Sep 19 2024	12.41	176.75	166.8	205.25	98.42
Sep 20 2024	27.48	177.73	168.65	206.47	98.98
Sep 21 2024	42.31	178.71	170.51	207.68	99.54
Sep 22 2024	56.8	179.69	172.37	208.9	100.1
Sep 23 2024	70.87	180.66	174.23	210.12	100.65
Sep 24 2024	84.53	181.64	176.08	211.34	101.2
Sep 25 2024	97.78	182.62	177.92	212.56	101.75
Sep 26 2024	110.66	183.6	179.76	213.78	102.29
Sep 27 2024	123.23	184.58	181.59	214.99	102.83
Sep 28 2024	135.54	185.56	183.4	216.21	103.37
Sep 29 2024	147.65	186.55	185.2	217.43	103.9
Sep 30 2024	159.62	187.53	186.99	218.64	104.43

	Moon	Sun	Mercury	Venus	Mars
Oct 1 2024	171.48	188.51	188.77	219.86	104.96
Oct 2 2024	183.28	189.5	190.53	221.08	105.48
Oct 3 2024	195.06	190.48	192.28	222.29	106
Oct 4 2024	206.86	191.47	194.02	223.51	106.51
Oct 5 2024	218.72	192.45	195.74	224.72	107.02
Oct 6 2024	230.66	193.44	197.45	225.94	107.53
Oct 7 2024	242.75	194.42	199.14	227.15	108.03
Oct 8 2024	255.03	195.41	200.82	228.37	108.53
Oct 9 2024	267.55	196.4	202.49	229.58	109.02
Oct 10 2024	280.37	197.39	204.15	230.79	109.51
Oct 11 2024	293.54	198.38	205.79	232.01	109.99
Oct 12 2024	307.11	199.37	207.42	233.22	110.47
Oct 13 2024	321.1	200.35	209.04	234.43	110.95
Oct 14 2024	335.5	201.34	210.64	235.64	111.42
Oct 15 2024	350.27	202.34	212.24	236.85	111.88
Oct 16 2024	5.31	203.33	213.82	238.06	112.34
Oct 17 2024	20.5	204.32	215.39	239.27	112.8
Oct 18 2024	35.69	205.31	216.95	240.48	113.25
Oct 19 2024	50.7	206.3	218.51	241.69	113.69
Oct 20 2024	65.4	207.3	220.05	242.9	114.13
Oct 21 2024	79.69	208.29	221.58	244.1	114.57
Oct 22 2024	93.51	209.29	223.1	245.31	115
Oct 23 2024	106.87	210.28	224.61	246.52	115.42
Oct 24 2024	119.79	211.28	226.11	247.72	115.84
Oct 25 2024	132.34	212.27	227.61	248.93	116.25
Oct 26 2024	144.58	213.27	229.09	250.14	116.66
Oct 27 2024	156.59	214.27	230.56	251.34	117.05
Oct 28 2024	168.46	215.27	232.02	252.54	117.45
Oct 29 2024	180.25	216.26	233.47	253.75	117.83
Oct 30 2024	192.02	217.26	234.91	254.95	118.22
Oct 31 2024	203.83	218.26	236.34	256.15	118.59

	Moon	Sun	Mercury	Venus	Mars
Nov 1 2024	215.71	219.26	237.76	257.36	118.96
Nov 2 2024	227.71	220.27	239.17	258.56	119.31
Nov 3 2024	239.84	221.27	240.56	259.76	119.67
Nov 4 2024	252.13	222.27	241.94	260.96	120.01
Nov 5 2024	264.6	223.27	243.31	262.16	120.35
Nov 6 2024	277.27	224.28	244.65	263.35	120.68
Nov 7 2024	290.17	225.28	245.98	264.55	121
Nov 8 2024	303.34	226.28	247.29	265.75	121.32
Nov 9 2024	316.8	227.29	248.58	266.94	121.62
Nov 10 2024	330.58	228.29	249.84	268.14	121.92
Nov 11 2024	344.7	229.3	251.08	269.33	122.21
Nov 12 2024	359.13	230.3	252.29	270.53	122.49
Nov 13 2024	13.85	231.31	253.46	271.72	122.76
Nov 14 2024	28.76	232.31	254.6	272.91	123.03
Nov 15 2024	43.76	233.32	255.69	274.1	123.28
Nov 16 2024	58.68	234.33	256.73	275.29	123.53
Nov 17 2024	73.38	235.34	257.72	276.47	123.76
Nov 18 2024	87.75	236.34	258.65	277.66	123.99
Nov 19 2024	101.68	237.35	259.51	278.85	124.2
Nov 20 2024	115.15	238.36	260.28	280.03	124.41
Nov 21 2024	128.17	239.37	260.97	281.21	124.61
Nov 22 2024	140.77	240.38	261.56	282.39	124.79
Nov 23 2024	153.03	241.39	262.04	283.57	124.97
Nov 24 2024	165.04	242.4	262.39	284.75	125.13
Nov 25 2024	176.89	243.41	262.61	285.93	125.28
Nov 26 2024	188.67	244.43	262.67	287.11	125.42
Nov 27 2024	200.45	245.44	262.57	288.28	125.55
Nov 28 2024	212.31	246.45	262.3	289.46	125.67
Nov 29 2024	224.31	247.46	261.85	290.63	125.78
Nov 30 2024	236.48	248.48	261.21	291.8	125.87

	Moon	Sun	Mercury	Venus	Mars
Dec 1 2024	248.85	249.49	260.39	292.97	125.95
Dec 2 2024	261.42	250.51	259.41	294.13	126.02
Dec 3 2024	274.21	251.52	258.27	295.3	126.08
Dec 4 2024	287.19	252.53	257.01	296.46	126.12
Dec 5 2024	300.36	253.55	255.67	297.62	126.15
Dec 6 2024	313.72	254.57	254.29	298.78	126.17
Dec 7 2024	327.26	255.58	252.92	299.94	126.17
Dec 8 2024	341	256.6	251.6	301.1	126.16
Dec 9 2024	354.94	257.61	250.38	302.25	126.14
Dec 10 2024	9.09	258.63	249.29	303.4	126.1
Dec 11 2024	23.43	259.64	248.35	304.55	126.05
Dec 12 2024	37.92	260.66	247.59	305.69	125.99
Dec 13 2024	52.49	261.68	247.02	306.84	125.91
Dec 14 2024	67.05	262.69	246.64	307.98	125.82
Dec 15 2024	81.48	263.71	246.43	309.11	125.71
Dec 16 2024	95.67	264.73	246.41	310.25	125.59
Dec 17 2024	109.51	265.74	246.54	311.38	125.46
Dec 18 2024	122.96	266.76	246.83	312.51	125.31
Dec 19 2024	136	267.78	247.25	313.64	125.15
Dec 20 2024	148.65	268.8	247.79	314.76	124.97
Dec 21 2024	160.95	269.82	248.44	315.88	124.78
Dec 22 2024	173	270.83	249.2	316.99	124.58
Dec 23 2024	184.87	271.85	250.03	318.1	124.36
Dec 24 2024	196.66	272.87	250.95	319.21	124.13
Dec 25 2024	208.47	273.89	251.93	320.32	123.89
Dec 26 2024	220.37	274.91	252.97	321.42	123.63
Dec 27 2024	232.45	275.93	254.07	322.52	123.37
Dec 28 2024	244.77	276.95	255.21	323.61	123.09
Dec 29 2024	257.35	277.97	256.39	324.7	122.79
Dec 30 2024	270.21	278.99	257.61	325.78	122.49
Dec 31 2024	283.34	280.01	258.86	326.86	122.17

APPENDIX B
Heliocentric Data

	Jupiter	Saturn	Uranus	Neptune	Pluto
Jan 1 2024	45.85	337.89	51.6	356.9	299.9
Jan 2 2024	45.94	337.93	51.62	356.91	299.9
Jan 3 2024	46.03	337.96	51.63	356.91	299.91
Jan 4 2024	46.12	337.99	51.64	356.92	299.91
Jan 5 2024	46.21	338.02	51.65	356.92	299.92
Jan 6 2024	46.31	338.05	51.66	356.93	299.92
Jan 7 2024	46.4	338.09	51.67	356.94	299.93
Jan 8 2024	46.49	338.12	51.68	356.94	299.93
Jan 9 2024	46.58	338.15	51.7	356.95	299.94
Jan 10 2024	46.67	338.18	51.71	356.95	299.94
Jan 11 2024	46.76	338.22	51.72	356.96	299.95
Jan 12 2024	46.85	338.25	51.73	356.97	299.95
Jan 13 2024	46.94	338.28	51.74	356.97	299.96
Jan 14 2024	47.03	338.31	51.75	356.98	299.96
Jan 15 2024	47.12	338.34	51.76	356.99	299.97
Jan 16 2024	47.21	338.38	51.77	356.99	299.97
Jan 17 2024	47.3	338.41	51.79	357	299.97
Jan 18 2024	47.39	338.44	51.8	357	299.98
Jan 19 2024	47.48	338.47	51.81	357.01	299.98
Jan 20 2024	47.57	338.51	51.82	357.02	299.99
Jan 21 2024	47.66	338.54	51.83	357.02	299.99
Jan 22 2024	47.75	338.57	51.84	357.03	300
Jan 23 2024	47.84	338.6	51.85	357.03	300
Jan 24 2024	47.93	338.63	51.86	357.04	300.01
Jan 25 2024	48.02	338.67	51.88	357.05	300.01
Jan 26 2024	48.11	338.7	51.89	357.05	300.02
Jan 27 2024	48.2	338.73	51.9	357.06	300.02
Jan 28 2024	48.29	338.76	51.91	357.06	300.03
Jan 29 2024	48.38	338.8	51.92	357.07	300.03
Jan 30 2024	48.47	338.83	51.93	357.08	300.04
Jan 31 2024	48.56	338.86	51.94	357.08	300.04

	Jupiter	Saturn	Uranus	Neptune	Pluto
Feb 1 2024	48.65	338.89	51.96	357.09	300.05
Feb 2 2024	48.74	338.92	51.97	357.1	300.05
Feb 3 2024	48.83	338.96	51.98	357.1	300.06
Feb 4 2024	48.92	338.99	51.99	357.11	300.06
Feb 5 2024	49.01	339.02	52	357.11	300.07
Feb 6 2024	49.1	339.05	52.01	357.12	300.07
Feb 7 2024	49.2	339.08	52.02	357.13	300.07
Feb 8 2024	49.29	339.12	52.03	357.13	300.08
Feb 9 2024	49.38	339.15	52.05	357.14	300.08
Feb 10 2024	49.47	339.18	52.06	357.14	300.09
Feb 11 2024	49.56	339.21	52.07	357.15	300.09
Feb 12 2024	49.65	339.25	52.08	357.16	300.1
Feb 13 2024	49.74	339.28	52.09	357.16	300.1
Feb 14 2024	49.83	339.31	52.1	357.17	300.11
Feb 15 2024	49.92	339.34	52.11	357.17	300.11
Feb 16 2024	50.01	339.37	52.12	357.18	300.12
Feb 17 2024	50.1	339.41	52.14	357.19	300.12
Feb 18 2024	50.19	339.44	52.15	357.19	300.13
Feb 19 2024	50.28	339.47	52.16	357.2	300.13
Feb 20 2024	50.37	339.5	52.17	357.21	300.14
Feb 21 2024	50.46	339.54	52.18	357.21	300.14
Feb 22 2024	50.55	339.57	52.19	357.22	300.15
Feb 23 2024	50.64	339.6	52.2	357.22	300.15
Feb 24 2024	50.73	339.63	52.21	357.23	300.16
Feb 25 2024	50.82	339.67	52.23	357.24	300.16
Feb 26 2024	50.91	339.7	52.24	357.24	300.16
Feb 27 2024	51	339.73	52.25	357.25	300.17
Feb 28 2024	51.09	339.76	52.26	357.25	300.17
Feb 29 2024	51.18	339.79	52.27	357.26	300.18

	Jupiter	Saturn	Uranus	Neptune	Pluto
Mar 1 2024	51.27	339.83	52.28	357.27	300.18
Mar 2 2024	51.36	339.86	52.29	357.27	300.19
Mar 3 2024	51.45	339.89	52.31	357.28	300.19
Mar 4 2024	51.54	339.92	52.32	357.28	300.2
Mar 5 2024	51.63	339.96	52.33	357.29	300.2
Mar 6 2024	51.72	339.99	52.34	357.3	300.21
Mar 7 2024	51.81	340.02	52.35	357.3	300.21
Mar 8 2024	51.9	340.05	52.36	357.31	300.22
Mar 9 2024	51.99	340.08	52.37	357.31	300.22
Mar 10 2024	52.08	340.12	52.38	357.32	300.23
Mar 11 2024	52.17	340.15	52.4	357.33	300.23
Mar 12 2024	52.26	340.18	52.41	357.33	300.24
Mar 13 2024	52.35	340.21	52.42	357.34	300.24
Mar 14 2024	52.44	340.25	52.43	357.35	300.25
Mar 15 2024	52.53	340.28	52.44	357.35	300.25
Mar 16 2024	52.62	340.31	52.45	357.36	300.25
Mar 17 2024	52.71	340.34	52.46	357.36	300.26
Mar 18 2024	52.8	340.37	52.47	357.37	300.26
Mar 19 2024	52.89	340.41	52.49	357.38	300.27
Mar 20 2024	52.98	340.44	52.5	357.38	300.27
Mar 21 2024	53.07	340.47	52.51	357.39	300.28
Mar 22 2024	53.16	340.5	52.52	357.39	300.28
Mar 23 2024	53.25	340.54	52.53	357.4	300.29
Mar 24 2024	53.33	340.57	52.54	357.41	300.29
Mar 25 2024	53.42	340.6	52.55	357.41	300.3
Mar 26 2024	53.51	340.63	52.56	357.42	300.3
Mar 27 2024	53.6	340.67	52.58	357.42	300.31
Mar 28 2024	53.69	340.7	52.59	357.43	300.31
Mar 29 2024	53.78	340.73	52.6	357.44	300.32
Mar 30 2024	53.87	340.76	52.61	357.44	300.32
Mar 31 2024	53.96	340.79	52.62	357.45	300.33

	Jupiter	Saturn	Uranus	Neptune	Pluto
Apr 1 2024	54.05	340.83	52.63	357.45	300.33
Apr 2 2024	54.14	340.86	52.64	357.46	300.34
Apr 3 2024	54.23	340.89	52.66	357.47	300.34
Apr 4 2024	54.32	340.92	52.67	357.47	300.34
Apr 5 2024	54.41	340.96	52.68	357.48	300.35
Apr 6 2024	54.5	340.99	52.69	357.49	300.35
Apr 7 2024	54.59	341.02	52.7	357.49	300.36
Apr 8 2024	54.68	341.05	52.71	357.5	300.36
Apr 9 2024	54.77	341.09	52.72	357.5	300.37
Apr 10 2024	54.86	341.12	52.73	357.51	300.37
Apr 11 2024	54.95	341.15	52.75	357.52	300.38
Apr 12 2024	55.04	341.18	52.76	357.52	300.38
Apr 13 2024	55.13	341.21	52.77	357.53	300.39
Apr 14 2024	55.22	341.25	52.78	357.53	300.39
Apr 15 2024	55.31	341.28	52.79	357.54	300.4
Apr 16 2024	55.4	341.31	52.8	357.55	300.4
Apr 17 2024	55.49	341.34	52.81	357.55	300.41
Apr 18 2024	55.58	341.38	52.82	357.56	300.41
Apr 19 2024	55.67	341.41	52.84	357.56	300.42
Apr 20 2024	55.76	341.44	52.85	357.57	300.42
Apr 21 2024	55.85	341.47	52.86	357.58	300.42
Apr 22 2024	55.94	341.51	52.87	357.58	300.43
Apr 23 2024	56.03	341.54	52.88	357.59	300.43
Apr 24 2024	56.11	341.57	52.89	357.6	300.44
Apr 25 2024	56.2	341.6	52.9	357.6	300.44
Apr 26 2024	56.29	341.64	52.91	357.61	300.45
Apr 27 2024	56.38	341.67	52.93	357.61	300.45
Apr 28 2024	56.47	341.7	52.94	357.62	300.46
Apr 29 2024	56.56	341.73	52.95	357.63	300.46
Apr 30 2024	56.65	341.77	52.96	357.63	300.47

	Jupiter	Saturn	Uranus	Neptune	Pluto
May 1 2024	56.74	341.8	52.97	357.64	300.47
May 2 2024	56.83	341.83	52.98	357.64	300.48
May 3 2024	56.92	341.86	52.99	357.65	300.48
May 4 2024	57.01	341.89	53.01	357.66	300.49
May 5 2024	57.1	341.93	53.02	357.66	300.49
May 6 2024	57.19	341.96	53.03	357.67	300.5
May 7 2024	57.28	341.99	53.04	357.67	300.5
May 8 2024	57.37	342.02	53.05	357.68	300.51
May 9 2024	57.46	342.06	53.06	357.69	300.51
May 10 2024	57.55	342.09	53.07	357.69	300.51
May 11 2024	57.64	342.12	53.08	357.7	300.52
May 12 2024	57.73	342.15	53.1	357.71	300.52
May 13 2024	57.81	342.19	53.11	357.71	300.53
May 14 2024	57.9	342.22	53.12	357.72	300.53
May 15 2024	57.99	342.25	53.13	357.72	300.54
May 16 2024	58.08	342.28	53.14	357.73	300.54
May 17 2024	58.17	342.32	53.15	357.74	300.55
May 18 2024	58.26	342.35	53.16	357.74	300.55
May 19 2024	58.35	342.38	53.18	357.75	300.56
May 20 2024	58.44	342.41	53.19	357.75	300.56
May 21 2024	58.53	342.45	53.2	357.76	300.57
May 22 2024	58.62	342.48	53.21	357.77	300.57
May 23 2024	58.71	342.51	53.22	357.77	300.58
May 24 2024	58.8	342.54	53.23	357.78	300.58
May 25 2024	58.89	342.58	53.24	357.78	300.59
May 26 2024	58.98	342.61	53.25	357.79	300.59
May 27 2024	59.07	342.64	53.27	357.8	300.6
May 28 2024	59.15	342.67	53.28	357.8	300.6
May 29 2024	59.24	342.7	53.29	357.81	300.6
May 30 2024	59.33	342.74	53.3	357.82	300.61
May 31 2024	59.42	342.77	53.31	357.82	300.61

	Jupiter	Saturn	Uranus	Neptune	Pluto
Jun 1 2024	59.51	342.8	53.32	357.83	300.62
Jun 2 2024	59.6	342.83	53.33	357.83	300.62
Jun 3 2024	59.69	342.87	53.34	357.84	300.63
Jun 4 2024	59.78	342.9	53.36	357.85	300.63
Jun 5 2024	59.87	342.93	53.37	357.85	300.64
Jun 6 2024	59.96	342.96	53.38	357.86	300.64
Jun 7 2024	60.05	343	53.39	357.86	300.65
Jun 8 2024	60.14	343.03	53.4	357.87	300.65
Jun 9 2024	60.22	343.06	53.41	357.88	300.66
Jun 10 2024	60.31	343.09	53.42	357.88	300.66
Jun 11 2024	60.4	343.13	53.44	357.89	300.67
Jun 12 2024	60.49	343.16	53.45	357.89	300.67
Jun 13 2024	60.58	343.19	53.46	357.9	300.68
Jun 14 2024	60.67	343.22	53.47	357.91	300.68
Jun 15 2024	60.76	343.26	53.48	357.91	300.69
Jun 16 2024	60.85	343.29	53.49	357.92	300.69
Jun 17 2024	60.94	343.32	53.5	357.92	300.69
Jun 18 2024	61.03	343.35	53.51	357.93	300.7
Jun 19 2024	61.12	343.39	53.53	357.94	300.7
Jun 20 2024	61.2	343.42	53.54	357.94	300.71
Jun 21 2024	61.29	343.45	53.55	357.95	300.71
Jun 22 2024	61.38	343.48	53.56	357.96	300.72
Jun 23 2024	61.47	343.52	53.57	357.96	300.72
Jun 24 2024	61.56	343.55	53.58	357.97	300.73
Jun 25 2024	61.65	343.58	53.59	357.97	300.73
Jun 26 2024	61.74	343.61	53.61	357.98	300.74
Jun 27 2024	61.83	343.65	53.62	357.99	300.74
Jun 28 2024	61.92	343.68	53.63	357.99	300.75
Jun 29 2024	62.01	343.71	53.64	358	300.75
Jun 30 2024	62.09	343.74	53.65	358	300.76

	Jupiter	Saturn	Uranus	Neptune	Pluto
Jul 1 2024	62.18	343.78	53.66	358.01	300.76
Jul 2 2024	62.27	343.81	53.67	358.02	300.77
Jul 3 2024	62.36	343.84	53.68	358.02	300.77
Jul 4 2024	62.45	343.87	53.7	358.03	300.78
Jul 5 2024	62.54	343.91	53.71	358.04	300.78
Jul 6 2024	62.63	343.94	53.72	358.04	300.78
Jul 7 2024	62.72	343.97	53.73	358.05	300.79
Jul 8 2024	62.81	344	53.74	358.05	300.79
Jul 9 2024	62.9	344.04	53.75	358.06	300.8
Jul 10 2024	62.98	344.07	53.76	358.07	300.8
Jul 11 2024	63.07	344.1	53.78	358.07	300.81
Jul 12 2024	63.16	344.13	53.79	358.08	300.81
Jul 13 2024	63.25	344.17	53.8	358.08	300.82
Jul 14 2024	63.34	344.2	53.81	358.09	300.82
Jul 15 2024	63.43	344.23	53.82	358.1	300.83
Jul 16 2024	63.52	344.26	53.83	358.1	300.83
Jul 17 2024	63.61	344.3	53.84	358.11	300.84
Jul 18 2024	63.69	344.33	53.85	358.11	300.84
Jul 19 2024	63.78	344.36	53.87	358.12	300.85
Jul 20 2024	63.87	344.39	53.88	358.13	300.85
Jul 21 2024	63.96	344.43	53.89	358.13	300.86
Jul 22 2024	64.05	344.46	53.9	358.14	300.86
Jul 23 2024	64.14	344.49	53.91	358.15	300.87
Jul 24 2024	64.23	344.52	53.92	358.15	300.87
Jul 25 2024	64.32	344.56	53.93	358.16	300.87
Jul 26 2024	64.4	344.59	53.95	358.16	300.88
Jul 27 2024	64.49	344.62	53.96	358.17	300.88
Jul 28 2024	64.58	344.65	53.97	358.18	300.89
Jul 29 2024	64.67	344.69	53.98	358.18	300.89
Jul 30 2024	64.76	344.72	53.99	358.19	300.9
Jul 31 2024	64.85	344.75	54	358.19	300.9

	Jupiter	Saturn	Uranus	Neptune	Pluto
Aug 1 2024	64.94	344.79	54.01	358.2	300.91
Aug 2 2024	65.02	344.82	54.02	358.21	300.91
Aug 3 2024	65.11	344.85	54.04	358.21	300.92
Aug 4 2024	65.2	344.88	54.05	358.22	300.92
Aug 5 2024	65.29	344.92	54.06	358.22	300.93
Aug 6 2024	65.38	344.95	54.07	358.23	300.93
Aug 7 2024	65.47	344.98	54.08	358.24	300.94
Aug 8 2024	65.56	345.01	54.09	358.24	300.94
Aug 9 2024	65.64	345.05	54.1	358.25	300.95
Aug 10 2024	65.73	345.08	54.12	358.25	300.95
Aug 11 2024	65.82	345.11	54.13	358.26	300.95
Aug 12 2024	65.91	345.14	54.14	358.27	300.96
Aug 13 2024	66	345.18	54.15	358.27	300.96
Aug 14 2024	66.09	345.21	54.16	358.28	300.97
Aug 15 2024	66.18	345.24	54.17	358.29	300.97
Aug 16 2024	66.26	345.27	54.18	358.29	300.98
Aug 17 2024	66.35	345.31	54.19	358.3	300.98
Aug 18 2024	66.44	345.34	54.21	358.3	300.99
Aug 19 2024	66.53	345.37	54.22	358.31	300.99
Aug 20 2024	66.62	345.4	54.23	358.32	301
Aug 21 2024	66.71	345.44	54.24	358.32	301
Aug 22 2024	66.79	345.47	54.25	358.33	301.01
Aug 23 2024	66.88	345.5	54.26	358.33	301.01
Aug 24 2024	66.97	345.53	54.27	358.34	301.02
Aug 25 2024	67.06	345.57	54.29	358.35	301.02
Aug 26 2024	67.15	345.6	54.3	358.35	301.03
Aug 27 2024	67.24	345.63	54.31	358.36	301.03
Aug 28 2024	67.33	345.66	54.32	358.36	301.03
Aug 29 2024	67.41	345.7	54.33	358.37	301.04
Aug 30 2024	67.5	345.73	54.34	358.38	301.04
Aug 31 2024	67.59	345.76	54.35	358.38	301.05

	Jupiter	Saturn	Uranus	Neptune	Pluto
Sep 1 2024	67.68	345.8	54.36	358.39	301.05
Sep 2 2024	67.77	345.83	54.38	358.4	301.06
Sep 3 2024	67.85	345.86	54.39	358.4	301.06
Sep 4 2024	67.94	345.89	54.4	358.41	301.07
Sep 5 2024	68.03	345.93	54.41	358.41	301.07
Sep 6 2024	68.12	345.96	54.42	358.42	301.08
Sep 7 2024	68.21	345.99	54.43	358.43	301.08
Sep 8 2024	68.3	346.02	54.44	358.43	301.09
Sep 9 2024	68.38	346.06	54.46	358.44	301.09
Sep 10 2024	68.47	346.09	54.47	358.44	301.1
Sep 11 2024	68.56	346.12	54.48	358.45	301.1
Sep 12 2024	68.65	346.15	54.49	358.46	301.11
Sep 13 2024	68.74	346.19	54.5	358.46	301.11
Sep 14 2024	68.83	346.22	54.51	358.47	301.11
Sep 15 2024	68.91	346.25	54.52	358.47	301.12
Sep 16 2024	69	346.28	54.53	358.48	301.12
Sep 17 2024	69.09	346.32	54.55	358.49	301.13
Sep 18 2024	69.18	346.35	54.56	358.49	301.13
Sep 19 2024	69.27	346.38	54.57	358.5	301.14
Sep 20 2024	69.35	346.41	54.58	358.5	301.14
Sep 21 2024	69.44	346.45	54.59	358.51	301.15
Sep 22 2024	69.53	346.48	54.6	358.52	301.15
Sep 23 2024	69.62	346.51	54.61	358.52	301.16
Sep 24 2024	69.71	346.55	54.63	358.53	301.16
Sep 25 2024	69.79	346.58	54.64	358.54	301.17
Sep 26 2024	69.88	346.61	54.65	358.54	301.17
Sep 27 2024	69.97	346.64	54.66	358.55	301.18
Sep 28 2024	70.06	346.68	54.67	358.55	301.18
Sep 29 2024	70.15	346.71	54.68	358.56	301.19
Sep 30 2024	70.23	346.74	54.69	358.57	301.19

	Jupiter	Saturn	Uranus	Neptune	Pluto
Oct 1 2024	70.32	346.77	54.7	358.57	301.19
Oct 2 2024	70.41	346.81	54.72	358.58	301.2
Oct 3 2024	70.5	346.84	54.73	358.58	301.2
Oct 4 2024	70.59	346.87	54.74	358.59	301.21
Oct 5 2024	70.67	346.9	54.75	358.6	301.21
Oct 6 2024	70.76	346.94	54.76	358.6	301.22
Oct 7 2024	70.85	346.97	54.77	358.61	301.22
Oct 8 2024	70.94	347	54.78	358.61	301.23
Oct 9 2024	71.03	347.04	54.79	358.62	301.23
Oct 10 2024	71.11	347.07	54.81	358.63	301.24
Oct 11 2024	71.2	347.1	54.82	358.63	301.24
Oct 12 2024	71.29	347.13	54.83	358.64	301.25
Oct 13 2024	71.38	347.17	54.84	358.65	301.25
Oct 14 2024	71.47	347.2	54.85	358.65	301.26
Oct 15 2024	71.55	347.23	54.86	358.66	301.26
Oct 16 2024	71.64	347.26	54.87	358.66	301.26
Oct 17 2024	71.73	347.3	54.89	358.67	301.27
Oct 18 2024	71.82	347.33	54.9	358.68	301.27
Oct 19 2024	71.9	347.36	54.91	358.68	301.28
Oct 20 2024	71.99	347.4	54.92	358.69	301.28
Oct 21 2024	72.08	347.43	54.93	358.69	301.29
Oct 22 2024	72.17	347.46	54.94	358.7	301.29
Oct 23 2024	72.26	347.49	54.95	358.71	301.3
Oct 24 2024	72.34	347.53	54.97	358.71	301.3
Oct 25 2024	72.43	347.56	54.98	358.72	301.31
Oct 26 2024	72.52	347.59	54.99	358.72	301.31
Oct 27 2024	72.61	347.62	55	358.73	301.32
Oct 28 2024	72.69	347.66	55.01	358.74	301.32
Oct 29 2024	72.78	347.69	55.02	358.74	301.33
Oct 30 2024	72.87	347.72	55.03	358.75	301.33
Oct 31 2024	72.96	347.76	55.04	358.75	301.34

	Jupiter	Saturn	Uranus	Neptune	Pluto
Nov 1 2024	73.04	347.79	55.06	358.76	301.34
Nov 2 2024	73.13	347.82	55.07	358.77	301.34
Nov 3 2024	73.22	347.85	55.08	358.77	301.35
Nov 4 2024	73.31	347.89	55.09	358.78	301.35
Nov 5 2024	73.4	347.92	55.1	358.79	301.36
Nov 6 2024	73.48	347.95	55.11	358.79	301.36
Nov 7 2024	73.57	347.98	55.12	358.8	301.37
Nov 8 2024	73.66	348.02	55.14	358.8	301.37
Nov 9 2024	73.75	348.05	55.15	358.81	301.38
Nov 10 2024	73.83	348.08	55.16	358.82	301.38
Nov 11 2024	73.92	348.12	55.17	358.82	301.39
Nov 12 2024	74.01	348.15	55.18	358.83	301.39
Nov 13 2024	74.1	348.18	55.19	358.83	301.4
Nov 14 2024	74.18	348.21	55.2	358.84	301.4
Nov 15 2024	74.27	348.25	55.21	358.85	301.41
Nov 16 2024	74.36	348.28	55.23	358.85	301.41
Nov 17 2024	74.45	348.31	55.24	358.86	301.42
Nov 18 2024	74.53	348.34	55.25	358.86	301.42
Nov 19 2024	74.62	348.38	55.26	358.87	301.42
Nov 20 2024	74.71	348.41	55.27	358.88	301.43
Nov 21 2024	74.8	348.44	55.28	358.88	301.43
Nov 22 2024	74.88	348.48	55.29	358.89	301.44
Nov 23 2024	74.97	348.51	55.31	358.9	301.44
Nov 24 2024	75.06	348.54	55.32	358.9	301.45
Nov 25 2024	75.15	348.57	55.33	358.91	301.45
Nov 26 2024	75.23	348.61	55.34	358.91	301.46
Nov 27 2024	75.32	348.64	55.35	358.92	301.46
Nov 28 2024	75.41	348.67	55.36	358.93	301.47
Nov 29 2024	75.5	348.71	55.37	358.93	301.47
Nov 30 2024	75.58	348.74	55.38	358.94	301.48

	Jupiter	Saturn	Uranus	Neptune	Pluto
Dec 1 2024	75.67	348.77	55.4	358.94	301.48
Dec 2 2024	75.76	348.8	55.41	358.95	301.49
Dec 3 2024	75.84	348.84	55.42	358.96	301.49
Dec 4 2024	75.93	348.87	55.43	358.96	301.5
Dec 5 2024	76.02	348.9	55.44	358.97	301.5
Dec 6 2024	76.11	348.94	55.45	358.97	301.5
Dec 7 2024	76.19	348.97	55.46	358.98	301.51
Dec 8 2024	76.28	349	55.48	358.99	301.51
Dec 9 2024	76.37	349.03	55.49	358.99	301.52
Dec 10 2024	76.46	349.07	55.5	359	301.52
Dec 11 2024	76.54	349.1	55.51	359.01	301.53
Dec 12 2024	76.63	349.13	55.52	359.01	301.53
Dec 13 2024	76.72	349.17	55.53	359.02	301.54
Dec 14 2024	76.8	349.2	55.54	359.02	301.54
Dec 15 2024	76.89	349.23	55.56	359.03	301.55
Dec 16 2024	76.98	349.26	55.57	359.04	301.55
Dec 17 2024	77.07	349.3	55.58	359.04	301.56
Dec 18 2024	77.15	349.33	55.59	359.05	301.56
Dec 19 2024	77.24	349.36	55.6	359.05	301.57
Dec 20 2024	77.33	349.4	55.61	359.06	301.57
Dec 21 2024	77.41	349.43	55.62	359.07	301.58
Dec 22 2024	77.5	349.46	55.63	359.07	301.58
Dec 23 2024	77.59	349.49	55.65	359.08	301.58
Dec 24 2024	77.68	349.53	55.66	359.08	301.59
Dec 25 2024	77.76	349.56	55.67	359.09	301.59
Dec 26 2024	77.85	349.59	55.68	359.1	301.6
Dec 27 2024	77.94	349.62	55.69	359.1	301.6
Dec 28 2024	78.02	349.66	55.7	359.11	301.61
Dec 29 2024	78.11	349.69	55.71	359.12	301.61
Dec 30 2024	78.2	349.72	55.73	359.12	301.62
Dec 31 2024	78.29	349.76	55.74	359.13	301.62

Printed in Great Britain
by Amazon

44993822R00155